The Rabbit in the Thorn Tree

Modern myths and urban legends of South Africa

ARTHUR GOLDSTUCK

Penguin Books

PENGUIN BOOKS

Published by the Penguin Group
27 Wrights Lane, London W8 5TZ, England
Viking Penguin Inc, 40 West 23rd Street, New York, New York 10010,
USA
Penguin Books Australia Ltd, Ringwood, Victoria, Australia
Penguin Books Canada Ltd, 2801 John Street, Markham, Ontario,
Canada LR3 1B4
Penguin Books (NZ) Ltd, 182-190 Wairau Road, Auckland 10,New
Zealand
Penguin Books, Amethyst Street, Theta Ext 1, Johannesburg, South
Africa

Penguin Books Ltd, Registered Offices: Harmondsworth, Middlesex,
England

First published by Penguin Books 1990

Second impression 1991

Copyright © Arthur Goldstuck 1990

ISBN 0 140 148078

Typeset by Graphicset
Printed and bound by Creda Press
Cover design by Hadaway Illustration & Design

Contents

1 WHAT IS AN URBAN LEGEND AND WHERE DO I BUY ONE?

So there's this guy who lives in Kingsway Mansions in Auckland Park. That's near the SABC, so you can always expect something kinky to be going on there.

Anyway, one night the most horrible screaming is heard coming from his flat. The neighbours don't want to check it out because, you know how it is, people don't like to get involved. But the screaming goes on, and eventually someone calls the cops. They break down the door and find this beautiful woman tied to a bed, stark naked, screaming blue murder. They rush over to untie her. 'No, no,' she shouts. 'Look in the cupboard.' So they open the cupboard and there lies this guy, unconscious, with a broken leg. And he's dressed in a Superman costume. Realisation dawns. He'd been planning to swoop down from the top of the cupboard for some kinky sex, when the top of the cupboard collapsed.

Does this story sound familiar? It should. It's happened, by my calculations, to about half the population of South Africa — if you were to believe every variation doing the rounds.

Many people firmly believe at least one version — the version they heard from a friend of a friend of a witness to the event.

Such is the nature of Urban Legends. Urban legends have just that edge of credibility that convinces people the story really happened. But, as in the Superman case, they are clearly part of a modern mythology that has emerged from the urban landscape. They are invariably repetitions of stories that supposedly happened to a 'friend of a friend'.

My initiation into the urban legend world was a book called *The Vanishing Hitchhiker and other American urban legends*, written in 1981 by Jan Harold Brunvand of the Department of English at Utah University.

Here I discovered well-travelled and well-seasoned variations of dozens of the 'true' stories I had heard during my school and university years. Some of them I had believed and accepted to have happened in my own town or my own country.

There it might have ended, except that I suddenly began to spot urban legends cropping up everywhere.

In conversation with friends, in newspaper reports, in radio talk shows.

It was absurd. It was bizarre. But it was happening, and I was fascinated.

Again, there it might have ended. But in 1985 a particular rumour, well known as a classic urban legend the world over, became the subject of a newspaper investigation in South Africa. It led in turn, for me, to an ongoing dispute with various acquaintances who insisted it had happened to a friend of a friend of theirs.

I was vindicated when the public investigation came to nothing (see Chapter 5). And my private adventure had just begun.

The beautiful thing about urban legends is that you don't have to buy them. People offer them for free, you pick them up in newspapers, you suddenly find one submerged in your dim memories of adolescence. They are stories so amazing, with such a powerful ring of truth, you want to believe them. Yet they are so strange or so bizarre or so unsettling or so funny, that you later wonder how you could have believed them in the first place.

They're easy to believe. They come from such credible sources. Newspapers, friends, mothers.

Urban legends are not to be confused with old wives'

2

tales, of course, or superstitions, or customs. They're more like an alternative oral tradition. Where traditional oral folklore tends to be passed down by the elders of the community, the tribe or the village, urban legends tend to filter from the bottom upwards — from adolescents, barflies, gossips and rumour-mongers. And from reputable sources as well.

But repute is hardly the hallmark of the urban legend.

So what are its hallmarks?

Urban legends can be identified possibly as much by their functions as by their structure or style.

A central function that oral folklore has served since speech began, and certainly that urban legends serve today, is that of the cautionary tale.

Urban legends are often warnings of the terrible things that can happen if you step out of line, if you don't perform the role that society or nature has determined for you, or if you don't act according to the rules that society has made — written or unwritten.

Urban legends hold terrible punishments for wayward wives, promiscuous teenagers, cheating husbands, and even for married couples who merely step outside the bounds of what is considered normal behaviour.

What horrible and bizarre fates urban legends have in store for those who step outside the moral boundaries of their peers!

Some urban legends are cautionary tales not in the sense of what they warn you not to do, but rather from the perspective of what kind of people, places or corporations are going to try to destroy you or your possessions. Such urban legends seem to help advance the cause of paranoia, racism, suspicion and fear.

They may sound tailormade for South Africa, but are in fact an international phenomenon. They also serve a sociological and psychological function, particularly in a changing society like that of South Africa.

Despite violence and tension, there is in this country a growing commitment among people of all races and creeds to a new, better, freer and more just society. It's astonishing how many of the people who just ten years ago would have shuddered at the thought of sharing entertainment facilities with members of other race groups, today actively encourage and applaud integration.

Yet is it not too much to expect that such transformations of attitude could be total in so short a time?

Leaving aside for the moment the extremist whites who continue to resist change, can the racist attitudes that enabled enforced segregation to be acceptable and desirable to South African whites for forty years just have evaporated overnight? Such hatred, for that is what it is in the final analysis, must leave subconscious residues, even scars.

At the risk of sounding like a pop psychologist, the subconscious mind needs to heal those scars. It needs to process the remaining vestiges of hatred and come to terms with them and, by facing them, get rid of them. Where the conscious mind goes, the subconscious often follows only reluctantly and usually with a struggle.

How many people start a sentence with, 'I'm not a racist, but ...'? They are sharing in that subconscious struggle. For them, urban legends provide a means of expressing their residual racism without actually being racist. However, these legends aren't expressly designed to reinforce racial stereotypes. Superficially, they are only horror or humour tales: stories told to intrigue and impress, to scare and to warn.

Yet below the surface they may be riddled with prejudice, stereotypes and dark, Freudian symbolism.

So what is there to stop someone inventing urban legends that express personal prejudices?

While researching this book, I was at first annoyed and then merely amused at how many people suggested I make up legends. As if urban legends are short stories or jokes that can be concocted and consciously spread. If there's a single urban legend that has been invented and disseminated by design, as an urban legend, and which has entered the international mainstream of urban legends, folklorists have yet to find the evidence.

Even people who claim that a particular legend actually happened to them are not necessarily the source of that legend. The fact that legend and reality do sometimes coincide does not necessarily make the reality a precursor to the legend. On the contrary, this merely reinforces the legend.

Inventing a legend? You can try. It shouldn't be too difficult. Legends have formulas. They have typical elements. It shouldn't be difficult to study their structure and replicate them. Perhaps, if you're lucky, in twenty years' time your story may be a fully fledged legend.

But it is no good making up a story and calling it a legend, because it isn't out there, mixing it with the rest of the subculture, being told and retold, being collected by folklorists, being pondered over by newspaper columnists or reporters, being used to scare children out of their sleep.

Making up an urban legend is like making up a fairy tale and pretending it came down with the Brothers Grimm.

On the other hand, it is not unusual to come across a story that seems to be an urban legend, and to claim it to be an urban legend, and then to realise it has nothing of the pedigree of a true legend.

Urban legends are readily confused with jokes so there is no reason why jokes shouldn't be confused with urban legends.

In my enthusiasm, I myself may well have mistaken some stories for urban legends, and they may well be revealed in time not to meet all the criteria.

This is not intended to be the definitive book on urban legends, but rather an introduction to a rich, varied and entertaining phenomenon, from a South African perspec-

5

tive.

Unfortunately, there is little precedent to go by. As this is the first study of its kind in this country, there is little raw material collected in published form. Such research as there is may well be lurking somewhere in the dusty halls of academia.

Whereas international collections are usually drawn from research by folklorists, this work relies extensively on the media. Largely because the concept of urban legend is still obscure in this country, magazines and newspapers are regularly taken in by a legend masquerading as a news story.

One of my purposes is to increase journalists' awareness of the need to check their facts, especially when they are of a dramatic, sensational or bizarre nature. The temptation to run this kind of story as quickly as possible is hard to resist — and often results in deep professional embarrassment.

Another purpose in writing this book is to create a greater awareness and, perhaps, establish a stronger tradition of urban legend reportage, so that eventually the urban legends of South Africa may share the international recognition they receive in folklore circles in places like Germany, England, Scandinavia and the United States.

The ideal would be to create an environment in which one does not have to start from scratch in researching such legends, Where we have a body of modern folklore at the ready, so to speak; where one has a tradition of urban legends, where we have a body of modern folklore at the ready, so to speak; where one has a tradition of urban

Why urban legends? Why not rural legends?

The term can be something of a misnomer. Urban legends do occur out in the country, but generally they emerge from the urban landscape, or at least the suburban landscape. They are heard and believed most often, in South Africa, in the cities, townships and suburbs. It has been suggested that they be renamed 'suburban legends', for that is what many of them really are.

Urban legends are the oral culture of the modern, relatively sophisticated city person. They may have roots in traditional folklore, but they are not the same thing.

In Africa it is an especially relevant issue. The oral tradition in conventional folklore is still very much alive on this continent and not only alive, but vibrant and highly relevant to its cultural life. Urban legends certainly cannot claim the same relevance, although scholars may some time in the future make a strong case for it. Indeed, there may well be an intersection between urban legends and oral tradition in African folklore. Some of the modern tales may well be ancient stories in the oral tradition that have evolved into 'new' urban legends.

The Rabbit in the Thorn Tree does not, however, concern itself with the current urban legend controversy among academics, where there are three distinct schools of thought with regard to folklore studies. One branch takes the approach that all legends should be traced back to original, ancient 'Ur' legends, identified by various motifs as true folklore. Another school of thought is more psycho-analytical, and is more concerned with analysing the meaning of legends. A third school believes legends can only be understood by the immediate sociological context in which they are told.

This book borrows from all three approaches where such borrowing improves appreciation of the legends, and clarifies their meaning or origin, but it does not claim to be an academic study.

It does not refer to indices of folk motifs, which a formal approach would demand.

However, my approach does not seem entirely alien to the attitude of some academics. Peter Esterhuysen, an oral literature specialist who has taught classes on urban legends at the University of the Witwatersrand, commented: 'I don't think it matters whether you find the original oral

7

legend, or whether in fact you find that the legend is true. What is important is that it is widely travelled, that there's something in the story which makes people transmit it in different variations. I don't think the identifiable motifs are as important as the "performance" of the legend.'

On that note, let the performance begin.

2 POLITICAL ANIMALS

Hunting for folklore in the murky world of politics, it is often difficult to distinguish between conspiracy theory and urban legend. The difference, perhaps, lies in whether one hears it from an obsessive paranoid or from the common man in the street.

Watch for hooded eyes shifting nervously from side to side, voice tight with an edge of panic, talking in hushed, confidential tones. You are probably listening to dark rumours about the Rockefellers, the Council for Foreign Relations, the Protocols of the Elders of Zion, the International Bankers' Conspiracy...

Urban legends are made of simpler stuff.

Conspiracy theories tend to be attractive largely to people who are by nature deeply suspicious of anything associated with money or organisation — any organisation.

Urban legends appeal to the more well-adjusted individual, the type of person who enjoys — and perhaps believes — a good rumour without accepting it as an article of faith.

Even so, in a politically volatile atmosphere, urban legends have a way of getting a little out of hand.

South Africa has always been a politically charged environment, particularly at times of great upheaval and change. The period leading from the South African War of 1899 up to the declaration of the Union of South Africa in 1910 was such a time. The same applies to the period from the start of World War II, which South Africa entered against the wishes of much of its Afrikaans population, up to the National Party election victory of 1948, which ushered in apartheid and all it stood for.

The 1990s are again such a time. The Nationalist Government has significantly 'loosened the screws', and has for the first time publicly acknowledged the need for blacks to share in the running of the country. The event has seemed inevitable since the mid-1970s, and it is in the period from 1976 to 1990 that most of the legends in this book — particularly the political legends — are set.

The Rabbit in the Thorn Tree

The archetypal South African political urban legend is the story of the Rabbit in the Thorn Tree.

On 30 September 1987, Barclays Bank, the largest financial institution in the country, formally changed its name to First National Bank. The parent company in the United Kingdom had disinvested, and the local subsidiary wanted a new image that would reflect its independence and identity as a South African bank.

The name change was preceded by a media campaign that cost R45-million, spent on advertising as well as on new signs, promotional material and, in particular, a new logo.

The bank decided on a very simple, symbolic logo. It featured a thorn tree, silhouetted against a rising sun, symbolising an African landscape and a new dawn. 'Symbol of life, strength, hope,' read the slogan.

By coincidence, the branches of the stylised tree formed the shape of a near perfect outline of the continent of Africa. It may have been intentional, but when it was pointed out, First National Bank spokesmen insisted it was a fluke. The symbolism was, however, entirely appropriate, and there the matter would have rested.

Unfortunately, some sharp-eyed individual (or perhaps several sharp-eyed individuals) spotted another coincidence: the shape of a leaping rabbit in the branches. Some argued that the shape more closely resembled a hare, but no one took notice of such semantics — since a sinister symbolism had been 'discovered' for the rabbit.

According to the legend mill — and no one was able to track down the source of the claim — the rabbit was one of the symbols of the African National Congress, then still a banned organisation, constantly vilified by the state media.

The allegation was taken very seriously by First National Bank. They had only recently shaken off accusations of being 'the ANC bank': while still called Barclays, they had provided a R100 000 overdraft to a Johannesburg businessman, Yusuf Surtee. He had used the money to pay for full-page advertisements in various newspapers, calling for the unbanning of the ANC.

Those were the paranoid post-Rubicon days, when then-president PW Botha tolerated no challenge to his worldview.

In this context he had said, as quoted by Rex Gibson in the *Sunday Star*, 'I have no objection to businessmen talking to me about political matters. I only object when they do this in a misguided manner.' It came, therefore, as no great surprise when Botha, a long-time adversary of Barclays MD Chris Ball, ordered a parliamentary inquiry into the bank's extension of credit for the benefit of the ANC.

Meanwhile, people clustered on sidewalks outside First National branches, pointing out imaginative shapes in the logo.

There was a rifle, aimed into the heart of Africa; there was a springbok leaping over Africa; there was a face of a crocodile, with unspeakably dark and dangerous implications.

Understandably, First National Bank was feeling a little sensitive.

The bank's public affairs chief, Jimmy McKenzie, told the *Star* that talk about the logo had caused the bank unnecessary trouble.

'All sorts of things are read into it. It is quite ridiculous,' he said. 'We were not aware there were these things in the tree until people started pointing them out. Apart from the "Africa", which we did notice, we did not see any of the other things.'

Without further ado, the bank redesigned its thorn tree, killing off all the rabbits, springbok and crocodiles. An entire continent disappeared beneath the artist's hands.

The bank would not admit, however, that public opinion had forced the change.

'What we have done with the tree, after an appeal from our own design unit, is just thicken the branches,' the *Star* quoted McKenzie as saying. 'Our design unit is creating new stationery, signs for branches ... and cuff links.

'In making the moulds for the production of the logos, they found that many of the branches were very flimsy and difficult to reproduce, so we refined the logo.'

But the legend wouldn't die. There was the matter of another crocodile, floating upside down at the top of the tree. And that rifle ...

FNB took a more forceful step. They published full-page advertisements in every mass-circulation Sunday newspaper, with a dramatic headline:

WE CALL ON ALL SOUTH AFRICANS TO REJECT THE MYTHS AND GOSSIP

We have noticed with interest the many positive comments made on the new logo of the Bank. However, we have also noted the speculation that the tree contained amongst other shapes a rabbit and that the rabbit is the emblem of a political group.

Some have even suggested that a rabbit was deliberately inserted for its alleged associations.

Although people have appeared to have found some 6 or 7 shapes there was no deliberate insertion of any

shapes in the tree. Moreover, South Africa's foremost
authority on the ANC, Dr Tom Lodge, advises us that
there is no association between the rabbit and the ANC.
     ... we do not support the ANC, nor do we support any
political organisations or parties. We are not the 'ANC
bank'.

The American Experience: the Procter & Gamble Logo

It would have been cold comfort for FNB to know that they
weren't the first corporation to land in hot water with myth-
mongers over a logo.

In a celebrated case in the United States, the giant Procter
& Gamble corporation also succumbed to change — after
holding out for more than fifty years.

Folklorist Jan Harold Brunvand documented the case in
The Choking Doberman, the second of four books he has
written on urban legends. He learned that the company had
in 1930 commissioned a sculptor to design its logo, which
shows the profile of an old man's face in a crescent moon,
facing a scattering of thirteen stars.

But the legend, as recounted by Brunvand, goes like this:

> *The moon-man and the 13 stars ... are really satanic*
> *symbols, and the appearance of the drawing on so many*
> *everyday products (toothpaste, detergent, diapers, soap)*
> *is alleged to be P&G's way of referring obliquely to its*
> *support of a demonic cult. Seemingly, everything about*
> *the trademark that can possibly be fit into this fantastic*
> *rumor has been 'explained'.*

The man in the moon's beard forms the number 666 — the
mythical mark of the Beast — if you read it backwards in a
mirror while looking at it from the corner of your eye. And

the stars, if connected in a certain way, form another 666. One claim linked it not to the antichrist, but to the Reverend Sun Myung Moon, founder of the Unification Church, popularly known as the 'Moonies'. Hence, obviously, a man in the moon.

Procter & Gamble were forced to fend off a series of campaigns against their logo. In 1980 the enquiries began to come in thick and fast, especially from Minnesota. Everyone wanted to know if the symbol meant that the company was supporting the 'Moonies' financially.

Enquiries then began to shift to the satanism story, and calls or letters rose from a few hundred a month to thousands.

In January 1982 the company sent out press releases to explain the origin of their trademark and, hopefully, quash the rumours. But news coverage only added fuel to the fire. By June of that year, 15 000 calls a month were coming in. Fifteen telephone operators were assigned full-time to deal with the calls.

Five prominent religious leaders, including Moral Majority founder Reverend Jerry Falwell, publicly stated that they were confident of P&G's innocence. Despite this, however, things got worse.

P&G even resorted to suing individuals who reported the myth as fact. They collected forty-two different variations of mimeographed pamphlets repeating the myth as true and warning the public not to buy P&G products.

Throughout the 1980s this pattern repeated itself. Periodically, P&G would take out adverts in major newspapers, denying the rumours and explaining the history of their logo.

Finally, like FNB, they gave in and simply changed their logo.

Indeed, since FNB culled their rabbit, they have heard hardly a mention of their former 'ANC bank' tag. Perhaps this is as much a product of their public relations efforts as of the changing political climate in South Africa.

The ANC is unbanned, operates legally within South Africa, and its banking connections are now largely irrelevant, at least from the legend point of view.

In fact, FNB now have a rival in the legend stakes, none other than their former 'partners'.

The ANC Bank Card

A legend seems to have emerged, fresh from the box, that the ANC has started its own bank, and provides its clients with bank cards in its official black, green and yellow colours. However, it has not proved easy to find an outlet of this bank. As is so often the case with new legends, I have the *Sunday Times* to thank for this report, from its political news page of 3 June 1990:

> *Agents from a mystery bank which they claim is linked to the ANC have been accepting fees and recruiting clients in the Western Cape.*
>
> *But a* Sunday Times *probe this week could find no official record of any 'African National Commercial Bank' or its offices.*
>
> *According to reports given to the* Sunday Times, *agents claiming to represent the bank are asking residents of Cape Town's townships to join the bank for a fee.*
>
> *Once the fee is paid, the 'client' is presented with a bank 'membership' card printed in black, yellow and green ANC colours.*

The report goes on to quote a vehement rejection of the bank by Amos Lengisi, an ANC Western Cape executive member. 'We disassociate ourselves completely from this bank — if it exists,' he said.

'Officials of the bank have been distributing information leaflets asking people to sign up for a fee ranging from R15 to R30. Lengisi told the *Sunday Times*. 'People who join get a card in our colours, but without our logo.'

Unfortunately, the *Sunday Times* was unable to provide evidence of the card's existence, nor of any individual who had been taken in by the alleged agents of the bank.

The report has remarkable parallels with another ANC legend doing the rounds, that of domestic workers who tell their employers they are paying the ANC a monthly rental which guarantees their taking over their employers' homes (see next chapter). The most significant difference is that the bank story seems to be spread largely in the townships, while the home-buying legend is very much a product of white suburbia.

In both cases, the immediate victims are supposedly gullible Africans. In both cases, newspaper reports do not quote or even name any of these victims. And finally, in both cases, after initial newspaper reports, no one has conducted an investigative follow-up.

This suggests that editors either recognise the stories for what they are, or that they tend to regard such stories as too tame for their readers. And who can blame them, considering some of the more lurid legends of this land?

The White Apocalypse

Top of the heap comes a tale which strikes at the very heart of white fears: on a certain day, the entire black population will rise up and kill as many whites as it can.

There were few South Africans who did not come into contact with the most recent product of this legend. An anonymous pamphlet went out, via fax machines, to every corner of South Africa, exhorting the black masses to strike at the white oppressors on 10 April 1990.

The pamphlet, titled 'AMANDLA!', with the subtitle 'Views and News of Blacks fighting for freedom in South Africa', conveniently incorporated two great myths. One half of the pamphlet was headed THE AIDS VIRUS IS A RACIST PLOT! (see Chapter 14) and the other UNITE AND RISE UP AGAINST WHITE DOMINATION.

The text of the latter read as follows:

Now that our leader Comrade Nelson Mandela is free, we must take what the whites stole from our ancestors hundreds of years ago. AMANDLA UWETHU! Power to the people! That will be our war cry. We will kill all the white racists and we will be free in Azania, free from oppression and discrimination!

COMRADE ... go to a white area today, go to a white man's house and ask to stay with him, he will call you a Kaffir, and chase you away.

The police are our enemy, we MUST rise up and take what belongs to us! Comrade Nelson told us to. We will attack the white racists in their houses built on the ruins of our ancestors' huts. FREE SOUTH AFRICA!

We all must get pangas, knives, guns, bricks and stones; anything that we can use to fight with and to destroy the white racists!

My black brother, go to a pretty white girl and ask her to go out with you, will she? NO! Why? Because you are black. We are better than the whites! That is why we are black. Idi Amin said so himself! Support your comrades in the ANC, kill an Indian or a coloured or a white today!

Finish what your ancestors and your fathers started. Comrade Nelson Mandela wants us to strike and riot! WE MUST OBEY HIM!

If we all strike on the 10th of April we will win our war against the whites! Go and choose your house in a white area today, when we win that house will be yours! WE MUST STRIKE ON THE 10TH OF APRIL!

There could be no better synthesis of all the worst paranoid nightmares of those white South Africans who do not accept the necessity of a non-racial society, and do not believe whites can survive in such a society.

The pamphlet was certainly not the result of ANC thinking. To start with, the ANC never refers to South Africa as Azania — that is a term employed by the black-consciousness movements, such as the Pan-Africanist Congress and the Azanian People's Organisation. The rhetoric is in fact in diametric opposition to the ANC's non-racial stance — but accords perfectly with the stereotype many uninformed whites have in their minds of the ANC.

It is also a common misconception in conservative circles that the ANC intends changing South Africa's name to Azania.

The use of Idi Amin's name to validate the pamphlet suggests a crude right-wing view of who might constitute a black authority figure — if it is not merely a poor attempt at a joke.

The pamphlet also adds grist to the mill of the legend that black people believe they will be able to choose their homes in white suburbs when the ANC comes to power.

The origin of the pamphlet, like so many in the land of urban legends, is impossible to determine. Most faxed copies seen by myself or my associates were sent by individuals who themselves had received them from people who wanted to show their friends the bizarre pamphlet that had been passed on to them by *their* friends.

The SA Police announced on 5 April 1990 that they were investigating the pamphlet, but that it was certainly a fake.

'These pamphlets are an amateurish effort which appears to be aimed at creating uncertainty and panic, especially among the white community,' said police public relations chief Major-General Herman Stadler. 'The SAP appeals to those groups mentioned not to become panicky, as this is exactly what the distributors of the pamphlets have in mind.'

Nelson Mandela himself dismissed the pamphlet as a 'smear' and completely contrary to the ANC's policy of non-racialism.

'There is no way the pamphlet was issued by anybody who is a member of the ANC,' he said, at the same time adding that he also did not believe it had been issued by the PAC.

Not coincidentally, 10 April was also the day before the first talks between the ANC and the South African Government were to have taken place to 'remove obstacles to negotiations'. As it happened the talks were postponed, and the timing of the pamphlet became irrelevant.

In a letter published in the *Star* on 3 May, prominent educationist Dr Franz Auerbach described the pamphlet as part of a 'campaign to sabotage the negotiation process, a campaign which deliberately increases suspicion, fear and hatred between white and black South Africans.'

A couple of months later the pamphlet had been all but forgotten.

We can be certain, however, that the myth about blacks rising up to kill the whites will return again and again, for it is yet another urban legend, tailormade for white fears on a black continent.

While this may be the first time it has appeared in pamphlet form, it is likely that the creators of the pamphlet had merely annexed a rumour that they themselves had heard from other sources.

In the bloody months leading up to PW Botha's declaration of a State of Emergency in June 1986, just such a call to destruction was a persistent rumour, although no specific date was ever mentioned.

It was also heard during the Vaal Triangle rent protests in 1984 — a period often referred to as the beginning of the mid-1980s 'cycle of unrest'. In September 1984, white schools throughout the Transvaal were put 'on alert', after rumours circulated that blacks had been instructed to attack every white school — allegedly because they had burnt down their own. The rumours — or, shall we say, urban legend — reached such hysterical proportions that newspapers had to publish disclaimers much like those following the 10 April 1990 fax.

After the 1961 Sharpeville massacre of black protesters by white police, the same kind of rumour was one of the motivations for the flood of white emigration from South Africa at the time, and, of course, the legend was especially current following the Soweto uprising of 16 June 1976.

I spent that year completing my final year of schooling at Brebner High in Bloemfontein. Although I did not keep a regular diary, I did record the occasional significant experience. Quite fortuitously, I recently discovered in my diary for 1976 the following entry, made on 31 August:

> *Van (the hostel master) called us in to discuss unrest in townships. He told us to form 3 groups of 11 (senior pupils) to defend the hostel in case of surprise attack. One of the men working at the hostel told Van that the blacks, mainly in Bochabela (township), were going on the rampage tomorrow and were going to kill as many whites as possible ... as usual, Van is tending to be dramatic.*

Predictably, the next day was as peaceful as any on the sleepy streets of Bloemfontein.

3

WHEN TRUTH IS STRANGER THAN LEGEND

Ever been at a party with people who know a thing or two about urban legends? They can make very poor guests. As you attempt to repeat a hair-raising experience that happened to a friend of someone you know, suddenly your story is shot down in flames by one of these oh-so-clever 'experts', who promptly introduce you to the meaning of 'urban legend'.

I've done my share of shooting down in my time ... and have had my share of egg thrown back in my face.

For instance, during an intimate dinner one evening, the mother of a friend expressed her shock as she recounted an experience of friends of her daughter-in-law's parents. Listening to her commence by reciting that complex chain of hearsay, my legend-alarm started jangling even before the story had begun. And this was the suspect tale:

The ANC Homebuyer

These friends of friends, who apparently lived in Pretoria, had a domestic servant who was not terribly well disposed towards her employers. One day she announced to them, out of the blue, that she would soon own their home. 'And how do you expect to do this?' they enquired, being *au fait* with the details of her breadline wages. 'I'm paying the ANC a rent of R10 a month, and when they take over the country, they'll give me the house,' she explained, quite earnestly.

21

As novel an approach as it might be to home mortgages, and as much as the ANC might require redistribution of land, this was patently absurd. I expressed my disbelief, as well as my appreciation for a brand new urban legend.

'But it's true!' insisted the speaker.

'So did they fire her?' I asked. 'Did they ask her for the identity of the local representative of the ANC Home Bonds division?'

The guest was stumped. With all protestations summarily silenced, I chalked up another one to the legends tally, satisfied and smug. For about 48 hours.

On 18 April 1990, the *Star* carried the following story on its front page:

BOGUS ANC FUND FOR DOMESTICS TO 'BUY' EMPLOYERS' HOMES

Several domestic workers have informed their employers in Durban and the Transvaal that their homes belong to the domestic workers who have contributed to an ANC fund.

Mr Tom Sebina, spokesman for the ANC in Lusaka, welcomed a police investigation into the 'criminal element who is defaming the ANC's name'.

'It is absolutely untrue that we have been collecting money from domestic workers for this purpose. The take-over of private homes has never been on the ANC's agenda.'

Mr Gordon Nixon of the Bluff is one of the surprised Durban residents to be told that his home no longer belonged to him.

'My wife and I went away for the weekend. When we returned yesterday, we found two well-dressed African gentlemen happily surveying my property and taking photographs. When I asked them what they were doing, they told me they had been paid R30 by my maid to take

photographs. They told me one picture goes to her and another to the "Mandela Fund".

'When I offered to introduce them to my shotgun or to call the police, they just laughed and said soon all white homes would belong to the people and to the ANC.'

Mr Nixon's domestic was dismissed on the spot and was not available for an interview today.

A similar scene took place when Mrs Shirley Aiston of Fynnland tried to sell her home. Her domestic, who had worked for her for 20 years, approached her and said she had been contributing to an ANC fund and the home belonged to her.

The same thing happened to a Cowie's Hill resident and to a Westville couple.

Captain R Bloomberg, media liaison spokesman for police headquarters in Pretoria, said today: 'We urge all domestic workers and employers to come forward with any information they may have so that we can investigate.'

He said this type of incident had also been reported on the Reef.

There, you may think, you have it. Names. Places. Official comment. Police investigations. Another legend bites the dust.

Or does it ...?

If ever I'd seen a questionable news report, this was one. No single individual who had actually paid money into a 'Mandela Fund', or to any such fund, was quoted. They were either 'unavailable for an interview' or quietly ignored.

The police response suggested that there wasn't enough actual evidence even to begin an investigation.

Mrs Aiston's maid struck me as being inordinately disloyal, considering her twenty years' service, unless this was countered by unusually low wages, as in my original exposure to the story.

The casual reference to 'a Cowie's Hill resident and to a Westville couple' was somewhat glib — and fairly typical of the manner in which news reporters are sometimes forced to treat hearsay.

I am not saying that all these people made up the story, nor am I saying it never happened. But the 'factual' stories are reported in a style so reminiscent of urban legend dissemination, and contain so many holes in their investigative foundations, I am forced to reserve my judgement.

And if it proves to be true after all?

Well, no one says an urban legend *has* to be entirely fictitious. Some of the great legends have their origin in fact; some *are* fact, but have gathered so much spurious detail as they roll along, it has become difficult to distinguish actuality from apocrypha.

Indeed, there may well be comprehensively documented reports of the ANC home bonds tale, complete with police reports, but even then, there is little doubt that the story has already passed into folklore, and is beginning to claim a firm place among the contemporary legends of South Africa. I have subsequently heard of it occurring in various locations in the Orange Free State and on the Witwatersrand. Several of the people who tell the story mention its appearance in the *Star*, mainly to back up their own new versions, but in fact indicating to what extent the report of a legend as fact can add further fuel to the legend itself.

I mentioned the phenomenon to an experienced journalist, who assured me that he had heard the same story in Zimbabwe shortly before that country's independence in 1980. One foreign correspondent told me it had actually happened in Zambia, and that the house had indeed come to be occupied by a former servant.

Clearly, it is a story tailormade for the South African condition as the country moves towards a society based on equality of the races, and as the disenfranchised black population begins to sense, for the first time, the arrival of a fair and just dispensation.

The story seems to sum up a conservative white perspective on the evolving society. It was heard at a time when the ANC was talking of the need to nationalise key industries, a concept which most whites, used to unbridled free enterprise, find disturbing, and who for decades succeeded in keeping black entrepreneurs out of the economic mainstream. While limited nationalisation would probably not seriously affect the average person in the street, the very concept has been portrayed by the media as alien to democracy and, by extension, to white interests. Even economic illiterates — and this includes a high proportion of the white population — can be heard railing against the very thought of a black-dominated government that may entertain the idea of nationalisation. This personal attitude to what is a largely corporate issue almost demands an outlet in a response that is meaningful to the individual. The ANC home bonds story fits the bill perfectly, for not only does it express fear of what the ANC has in store for whites, it also carries the subtle suggestion that blacks lack the intelligence to spot an obvious confidence trick when they are confronted with it.

There are several grounds for believing that the reports serve this purpose, rather than being a true account of a confidence trick.

Firstly, the question begs itself: if so many people are paying a regular fee to someone, there must be a means of making regular contact with the recipient of the money. Yet not a single domestic worker seems to have been questioned by police on this particular subject. It is unlikely that domestic workers would — or would want to — hold out against police questioning on such an issue. After all, from the reports, it seems as if they thought they had been engaged in legitimate commerce.

Then there is the matter of the police investigations. The very fact that a police spokesman has asked people to come forward with information so that the police can begin investigations suggests that they have no information to begin with, an unlikely situation if these eve^{...}ts really were occurring. Few home owners would hesitate to report such an incident to the police, particularly as they seem to have so little compunction in firing their domestic workers for what appears to be a situation in which the employees are victims.

And then there are the 'foreign' versions of the story.

Besides verbal corroboration from journalists of other southern African rumours of the tale, I received another, written, account of a very similar event that occurred while Namibia was moving towards independence in 1989.

> I have a cousin who lives in Grootfontein, Namibia. A few years ago she had a beautiful house built, which ranked as one of the most impressive houses in Grootfontein.
>
> One day she was approached by three Ovambos who said they were interested in buying her house. They walked through the entire house, lingering in every room, scrutinising everything. They asked her her selling price and, when she told them, laughed uproariously and said: 'Look after the house well, because in a year's time it will be ours for nothing.'

Today Namibia is independent, and my correspondent's cousin is, I am told, still happily living in her house.

Another Namibian story I was told in a fleeting conversation was an event which occurred in 1989 in the capital, Windhoek, at the time of the first free elections in Namibia. A large black family arrived at the home of a white resident, quite out of the blue, and camped out on his lawn. He demanded that they move off, but they refused.

They informed him that they had been allocated this house, and after the elections would move into it.

According to the narrator, the resident had had to call in the police, who evicted the family. The story was reported in the Namibian newspapers, I am told, but I have been unable to confirm this — not that I expected to. While neither of these versions includes a domestic worker, the stories serve the same purpose, and provide the same messages, and are clearly part of the same family of urban legends.

As I have suggested, there is still the possibility that the legend is based on fact but, to borrow from one of the unofficial philosophies of sub-editors at a well-known Sunday newspaper, why let the facts interfere with a good legend?

4 STATE DEPARTMENT

Routine as their presence may seem in political legends, the ANC are not the only inspiration for South Africa's more topical urban legends. The South African Government, along with the apparatus of state security and state departments in its many guises, is the butt of a fair share of legends.

Usually, government legends deal with outrageous extremities of bureaucratic red tape and absurd decisions made by officials.

South Africans have come to accept such stories as part of the fabric of their lives. After all, the amazing level of double-talk employed to explain apartheid for forty years has conditioned the public to suspend its credibility almost indefinitely.

The Mint of the Living Dead

Perhaps the most chilling of these government legends is the belief that people condemned to death are never really hanged.

They are led from their death-row cells, not to the gallows, but to the State Mint. Here they are put to work for the rest of their natural lives, making the coins that are supplied to banks, under conditions of pure slavery.

Why the Mint?

'Because the Government will never hang someone who can make money for them,' is the traditional explanation, with its unintentional pun.

Ina van der Linde, a writer for the weekly newspaper

Vrye Weekblad, aired this legend in a report on the temporary suspension of the death sentence in South Africa. She had visited the Mamelodi township cemetery, where the graveyard team from Pretoria Central prison offloaded the bodies of executed prisoners for burial:

> *We asked the caretaker where the condemned were buried. We drove up and down along the rows of graves. At the end of the cemetery he climbed out and pointed to a patch of overgrown ground. Three barely discernible mounds. He had forgotten their names. He could also not remember why they had been hanged ...*
>
> *A reason for the existence of the myth (about the Mint) is that the family is never allowed to see the body of an executed person.*
>
> *About an hour after the execution, the family is allowed to attend a service in the prison chapel. The coffin is placed in the front of the room. The family may not see the corpse, and they may not attend the funeral. It takes place immediately after the service. The coffins are taken to the cemetery by a black taxi-bus.*
>
> *Days or even weeks after the funeral, the prison authorities send a note to the family giving the number of the grave.*

Even without the tale about the Mint, this sounds like rich source material for urban legends. The body that is never seen, the funeral that is never witnessed, the mysterious black taxi that takes the body to its grave; it would be surprising if there *weren't* dark legends surrounding the death penalty.

Joyce Ozynski, organiser of the Anti-Censorship Action Group, told me she'd first heard the legend several years ago:

'When I heard it, I thought it was so weird. But you look at it: the graveyard is in a very obscure place. There are no tombstones. If your son is sentenced to death, for instance, and you want to visit his grave, the police put tremendous obstacles in your way.'

The British adult comic book *Crisis* recognised the story and its context as a powerful vehicle for a human rights statement. In their 3 March 1990 issue, produced in conjunction with Amnesty International and Art & Society, one third of the comic is devoted to a story called 'THE DEATH FACTORY'.

It tells of a death-row prisoner who dreams he is hanged. Instead of the noose tightening around his neck, however, he falls through the trapdoor of the scaffold into a pit below.

He is shocked to see there his fellow condemned prisoners, alive. A policeman orders him to 'join the others'. They walk down a tunnel and emerge in 'a subterranean hell ... a secret underground mint ... where you make money for the government — forever'.

The prisoner wakes up and realises the Mint is just a mint after all, and the legend is 'believed in by many black South Africans to ease the pain of losing loved ones'.

Folklorists would find the story somewhat unusual. Unlike many urban legends, which act in one way or another as cautionary tales, this is at first glance a story intended for comfort. However, it is told as often among middle-class whites, with a flavour closer to that of horror stories, and the context of the telling is usually a late-night 'chill-contest', somewhere along the lines of, 'You think that's scary, wait till you hear the one about how they really make our money ...'

Government legends as told from a white perspective are as often amusing as tragic. They seem designed to confirm long-held suspicions about officials meddling in our lives, or of Government incompetence.

30

The Short Filing Clerk

The next example was told to me by a former teacher, who had herself heard it from a former school secretary. It was repeated in March 1990, shortly after a scandal, aired in the press, about teachers not receiving their Government salaries for the month of January:

As far as I know, this really happened. It's about the TED (Transvaal Education Department). A teacher at Orange Grove Primary School received no salary cheque for three months. After the first month, she made enquiries. The Department told her they had no record of her — although she'd been teaching for seven years and had received a cheque every month up till then.

She had no choice but to wait and see what happened the next month. But the following month, she again didn't get her salary. She wrote letters, sent telegrams and telephoned the Department.

Still they insisted they had no record of her. So she went to the headquarters herself, and showed them all her documentation, basically proving her case. They finally admitted she had a point, but still vowed they had no record of her.

Finally, two days before the end of the third month, she received a call from the TED. They had found her file.

It turned out that one of their clerks, who was much shorter than the other clerks, had battled to reach her typewriter when she was sitting at her desk. So she had taken the nearest practical item — which happened to be a stack of files — and used them as a cushion ... I don't know how many other teachers were missing their salaries at the same time.

The story is a delightful amalgamation of prejudices

involving Government departments. State officials, according to the legend, are absurdly incompetent, they are obstinate to the point of denying the evidence before their eyes, they are grossly insensitive, they force their victims into the poorhouse ... and some of them are of less than average height.

In the context of the very real complaints about unpaid salaries, the legend has a strong ring of plausibility. Official spokesmen as much as said in the press that they didn't see the salary situation as a problem, and therefore did not see why the teachers should see it as a problem. Even urban legends have a hard time matching such glibness.

It is easy to see how, in this climate, a legend could emerge among teachers to reveal just how incompetent the education authorities can be.

The Killer Potato

The legend of the killer potato is told almost exclusively in the townships, and openly ridicules the victims, the SA Defence Force:

One day during the 1976 Soweto uprising, when the army was occupying the townships, a gang of Soweto kids lay in wait at a street corner. Their patience was rewarded for soon an armoured car, on patrol through Soweto, rolled round the corner, with a soldier sitting in the turret. One of the boys took a potato, cunningly painted army green, and lobbed it at the vehicle, hand-grenade style. His aim was true. Into the turret it went and rolled down into the cabin. The soldiers inside all scrambled out, and ran for their lives — minus their rifles. The youths quickly jumped in, and drove off with the vehicle and the rifles. The story was, of course, hushed up by the army.

There you have it: the ingenuity of township kids, who have learned about life the hard way, in a war situation, putting into practice what they have learnt, so those white soldiers had better watch out; the stupidity of the white soldiers, who are so nervous they'll fall for any old trick; and finally, the vulnerability of military vehicles — whereas they are in fact a source of terror and a symbol of state-sanctioned violence in the townships.

The legend thus serves to bolster confidence among township youth and render the armed white 'invaders' less threatening. A fascinating aspect of the legend is that it could have been told during any military occupation involving local resistance — 1960s Saigon or 1940s France, for instance.

The Sinister Chandelier

A legend which has been around for many years, usually in the form of a joke, is that of the sinister chandelier. Diplomats stationed in Russia, who are convinced the KGB is eavesdropping on them, are most often the protagonists. However, at the height of PW Botha's 'securocrat' rule — during which the various state security bodies were virtually given the run of the country — it suddenly emerged as an urban legend told about South Africa among foreign diplomats. It was said to have happened in the 1970s, when the notorious Bureau of State Security, or BOSS, was a byword for 'Big Brother' watching us:

Two diplomats arrived in South Africa to begin a tour of duty. They were put up at the President Hotel in Johannesburg on the night of their arrival. They had been warned that BOSS would be watching their every move, and that their hotel room would probably be bugged. Having previously been stationed in countries more repressive than South Africa, however, such warnings were a big joke to them.

As they unpacked in their room on the first floor, they discussed possible ways in which BOSS might be monitoring them. On impulse, they decided to search the room for secret transmitters or 'bugs'.

They searched the room from top to bottom, examining the telephone mouthpiece, the lampshade, the air conditioner, shelves and drawers, and the top of cupboards. Finally, one of them noticed a suspicious looking bulge in the carpet under one of the beds.

They pushed the bed aside, rolled up the carpet, and bingo: there was a strange little box, screwed into the floor.

One of them happened to have a screwdriver in his luggage, and they set to work on the box. Four inordinately large screws held it in place, and these they painstakingly removed, one at a time.

Finally, the box came loose from the floor. They discovered that they had in their hands ... a box. It had no apparent purpose but to hold the screws. It had another hole for a large screw in the bottom, but no electronic components at all.

Puzzled, they screwed the box back in place, rolled down the carpet and went downstairs to get something to eat. The hotel was in an uproar and they found the dining room had been closed off. Diners had apparently narrowly escaped tragedy when the huge chandelier in the ceiling had suddenly and mysteriously come loose and plummeted to the floor.

This legend has an air of authenticity — which confirms that it is a legend, rather than a joke — by the fact that the President Hotel was indeed a favoured venue for putting up diplomats in Johannesburg in the 1970s. (In later years they would be accommodated at other well-known city hotels.) If the story had been contrived merely to amuse, topicality would have demanded it be set in one of these newer venues.

While the legend does not make the Government the direct butt, but rather places diplomats in the role of the transgressors, the very flavour of the legend is an indictment of the Government: it has created such an aura of suspicion and paranoia that it has become perfectly natural for visitors to the country — not to mention South Africans themselves — to speculate on surveillance methods the Government may be using on them. Innocent civilians almost suffer the consequences of this climate of paranoia.

The suspicion of the two characters in the legend turns out to have been unfounded, and indeed dangerous. Yet, as with the Russian version, it does not suggest that the state security service is harmless — merely that one should not expect too much of it.

In a very different context, the next legend leads us to a similar conclusion, except that in this case it is the prison services which fall down on the job — literally!

The Clever Escape

A woman prisoner at one of the gaols in the Transvaal thought she had planned an ingenious escape. She worked in the carpentry shop, and she noticed that every time someone died in the prison, the chapel bells would ring and a coffin would be fetched from the workshop. Then the coffin would be brought back, with the body inside, and it would be nailed shut before being taken for burial.

The woman got friendly with the warder who supervised the burials, and eventually persuaded him to take a bribe. The deal was, next time someone died, he wouldn't have the coffin nailed shut immediately, but would give her a chance to climb in. He would then supervise the burial as usual. Later that night he would come back alone, dig up the coffin and let her out.

Everything went according to plan. One evening the bells rang, and she made her way to the workshop, her pockets stuffed with supplies — biscuits, a piece of biltong and a penlight torch. Although it was dark, she did not want to draw attention to herself by switching on a light. She could just make out the shape of the coffin in the shadowy gloom of the workshop.

Sure enough, the lid was still open. She quickly climbed inside and squeezed in next to the body. Before long, someone came along and nailed the coffin shut. It was lifted and carried out to a vehicle. Then followed a bumpy ride to the prison cemetery. The dead body was squeezed tightly against her, but she didn't dare move in case someone heard her.

Finally, the coffin was lowered into a pre-prepared grave, and it was covered with earth.

When she was sure no one would hear anything, she finally dared to move. Eager for some light, she took out her torch. She was curious to see whose coffin she was sharing, and shone the light on the dead person's face.

It was the warder she had bribed.

5 SHOPPING FOR LEGENDS

Rarely has one word struck so much terror into the hearts of South African parents as 'kidnap'. The highly publicised abduction of six young girls from white suburban areas during 1988 and 1989, and the subsequent linking of five of them to Cornelius van Rooyen, a known paedophile who killed himself minutes before police caught up with him, has made it one of the most emotive issues in South African society. Only political feelings elicit the same high level of response.

Yet, as serious and tragic as child kidnappings are, the anguish of the issue can be swamped by paranoia and melodrama. Let's sift the fact from the urban legend.

Sex Slaves of the Oriental

During the first half of 1985, the *Star* newspaper apparently carried a report which I have subsequently attempted to track down but without success. The gist of it was that a woman had phoned the *Star* in a state of near hysteria. She told them that a friend of hers had been kidnapped at the Oriental Plaza, the shopping mall created in west Johannesburg for Indian traders.

Her friend, a blonde, had gone into a changeroom, and had simply disappeared.

The caller had subsequently heard of four other women who had been kidnapped at the Oriental Plaza. They were being drugged and smuggled out of the country to be sold to Arabs in a white slavery plot. It was happening all the time and the police knew about it, she said, but they refused to do anything. She was not only upset, wrote the reporter, she was also extremely angry and highly indignant.

There was one other thing: she refused to give the newspaper the names of any of the kidnapped people. The police had the names, she said.

The *Star* naturally followed up the story, and phoned no less than fifty-two police stations around the Johannesburg and Witwatersrand area. Only one police spokesman had even heard of the story, but he said that investigations had shown there was no truth to it.

Any student of urban legends could have saved the *Star* a lot of time and trouble. The legend has been told in endless variations in the United States. As in South Africa, journalists have repeatedly been called upon by hysterical public pressure to pursue the rumours.

In Madison, Wisconsin, the local newspaper, *Capital Times*, ran a story on 10 November 1980, headlined:

ABDUCTION RUMORS HAVE POLICE PUZZLED.

The report included several classic ingredients:

> *Madison police and shopping center officials are becoming increasingly disturbed over a plague of rumors circulating that young girls are being drugged and abducted from shopping centers.*
>
> *The rumors began circulating about five weeks ago when a story made the rounds that a teenage girl was shot full of heroin in a restroom at West Towne (a shopping centre), and was being carried away by two women when she was rescued by relatives and taken to a hospital for treatment ...*

That story was repeated again and again, only the locations shifting ...

Members of the public inundated police with calls about the alleged incident, but they still only came up with third- and fourth-hand information. As with the Oriental Plaza legend, not a single name of a witness or relative — let alone a victim — was ever supplied.

Jan Brunvand records in *The Choking Doberman* that flare-ups of the story in the past decade have occurred in Minneapolis, Sioux City, and Council Bluffs (Iowa), 'but hardly an urban center in the United States that is large enough to have suburbs and shopping centers has been free of it'. The victims are usually blonde — and they're usually kidnapped for a prostitution racket.

In South Africa I have found three distinct strands of the legend where the location is the Oriental Plaza. The most common is the version reported to the *Star*: young women, particularly blondes, go into the changerooms in Oriental Plaza clothing shops, and never come out again. They've been kidnapped and shipped off to the Middle East as part of the white slave trade.

The second version mentions a specific shop in the Plaza: 'that little store that sells scarves'. Women are told not to go to the Oriental Plaza alone, as they'll be sold into prostitution in the Middle East. The scarf shop is a 'supply centre' for the trade: 'people go in there and just disappear'.

The third variety refers to a carpet shop — of which there are several in the Plaza. Apparently, as young women walk among the forests of pillars created by the rolled-up carpets, they are suddenly pulled in among the carpets. They are then drugged, rolled up in a carpet and smuggled out of the country to be sold as slaves in the Middle East.

These versions have all been pulled together in one all-embracing version, which has it that 'when you go into the changerooms in any of the clothes shops, they wait for you to take off your clothes. Then they grab you, inject you with drugs, wrap you up in a carpet, and smuggle you out of the country.'

At the height of the 'scare', in 1985, I raised the matter at a dinner table one night. Before I could reach the part where I spoil everyone's fun by announcing that a similar story has been told with regard to just about every shopping mall in the world, the hostess chimed in: 'I know one of the people it happened to.'

I immediately demanded names, places, dates. The hostess said she'd have to check her facts and come back to me. When I suggested that this was already beginning to sound like an urban legend, I was fixed with an icy glare, followed by a lecture on the perils facing young women in these tense times.

Nevertheless, she did begin to look into the matter, and shortly afterwards informed me she had been slightly mistaken: it was a woman who worked with a cousin of her husband who knew the woman who had been kidnapped. I repeated my assertion that it was an urban legend and was subjected to another hostile lecture. She then insisted she would get the name for me. A year later, she was still insisting — and so were several other acquaintances, always female, who castigated me furiously as a typical cynical male.

(So vehement were the responses, I decided to begin researching urban legends more thoroughly, and this book is an indirect result.)

Why all this passion?

It appears that not only do the fearful implications of kidnapping raise some people's blood pressure, but also the idea that someone might not believe the story, and by implication not accept the warning that it is dangerous to go to these shopping malls.

This is a common attitude in the land of urban legends, but this tale has an additional resonance, and one that is especially relevant in South Africa.

Where the Chinese community is plagued by cat bone libels (see Chapter 10), South Africa's Indian community must now cope with the kidnap libel. It should be seen in the context that, added to the many racist and racial confusions besetting this country, there is the suspicion that many blacks and whites seem to have of Indian traders. It is related to the common and notorious myths about Jewish businessmen, but suffers additionally from Indians having been forced over the years into 'commercial ghettos'.

Johannesburg suburbs like Pageview and Vrededorp were traditional Indian communities before they were reproclaimed white areas under the infamous Group Areas Act. When Indian businessmen resisted moving out of these suburbs, the Government offered them a very expensive carrot: an ultra-modern shopping complex in nearby Fordsburg. It was to be called the Oriental Plaza.

Beside the fact that the name smacked of typical Government patronisation, the move was seen as an attempt to co-opt Indian business into Government thinking, and most traders at first resisted. It soon became clear, however, that they had little choice in the matter. After an initial boycott, the centre in time became the mecca of Indian trade in Johannesburg, patronised by people of all races.

For all the initial sterility of the Plaza's structure, the shopkeepers have managed to add to the centre a vibrance and colour that brings to Johannesburg a strong flavour of the East. Or what white suburbanites imagine to be the East. Nevertheless, while it is hardly a typical Arab bazaar, it has its evocations thereof and that, to many South Africans, is a subconscious source of fear, suspicion and paranoia. For have we not seen in adventure movies about the Middle East just how dangerous Arab markets are? Have we not heard news reports of tourists stabbed in the bazaars? Have we not come to accept these as dens of vice, murder or ... worse?

Well, some of us have.

Barre Tolken, author of *The Dynamics of Folklore,* calls

such legends 'the international minority conspiracy'. It appeals to the worldview of anyone who has an open or latent suspicion of minorities. It finds especially fertile ground in South Africa.

As suggested before, such legends not only confirm the prejudices of overt racists, but enable people to face up to their subconscious racial prejudices without having to admit to these prejudices. A psychoanalyst might say it makes for greater inner harmony, and by extension allows for the eventual elimination of such unhealthy attitudes.

Sound too neat?

Urban legends by their nature are usually far too neat for comfort. Their meanings and functions seem tailormade for psychological pigeonholes. By way of illustration, try this shopping centre legend, most recently attributed by a Boksburg resident to Eastgate, shopping mecca for the East Rand.

Terror in the Toilets

I have been warned never to go alone into the toilets at Eastgate after the experience of a woman who went shopping there with her son. While she was shopping he wanted to go to the toilet. She was carrying a lot of bags, so she let him go alone into the men's cloakroom. She waited and waited and he didn't come out. Eventually she asked a security guard to go in and check up on her son. He went in and found the boy lying in a pool of blood. His penis had been cut off, apparently by a gang of 'Coloured' boys.

The implications — the meanings and the menace — are so clear, they hardly bear discussion. In the United States the legend is known as The Mutilated Boy, and it causes emotional hysteria in the most level-headed of people. It awakens the average parents' darkest fears about the well-being of their children.

Where the changeroom kidnappings of blondes provides a dire warning for daughters, the Terror in the Toilets does the trick for sons.

These legends scream their cautions at children and young people: do not go into changerooms or restrooms in strange shopping malls — at least if you are by yourself.

It warns parents: do not allow your children to wander off alone.

The legends thus serve the most basic oral tradition of Cautionary Tale, while providing a 'safe' outlet for racial prejudice.

As Barre Tolken puts it, 'Watch out for these people, they're out to get us and they'll be likely to attack us in the most vulnerable places and the most objectionable ways.'

Jan Brunvand adds to this comment: '...and they'll also strike without warning in the settings of our simple pleasures or in our "safe" middle-class centers of commerce.'

Brunvand points to dramatic links between these legends and the medieval 'blood libel', whereby Jews were constantly accused of torturing and murdering Christian children as a Passover sacrifice. In the days of the Roman Empire, the shoe was on the Christian foot, with Romans accusing them of murdering Jewish children in Christian initiation rites. Hitler himself used the blood libel as one of his justifications for the Holocaust.

Even today, it persists. On 27 August 1990, the *Daily Mail* carried a feature syndicated from the *Washington Post*, under the headline 'Poland invents a new form of racism: anti-Semitism without the Jews'.

It examined the manner in which anti-Semitism can break out even in a community which has very few Jews, largely because of the need to find scapegoats for the nation's economic decline. Writer Blaine Harden reported:

...Poland's Catholic church is preparing an unpreceden-

ted document to be sent this fall to every parish in this overwhelmingly Catholic country.

Members of the Polish Episcopate Commission for Dialogue with Jews say the document will instruct priests and nuns to confront and dispel anti-Semitic folk beliefs.

One such belief that persists in some rural areas is that Jews kidnap Catholic children and use their blood to make unleavened bread...

Abduction, with Trim and Dye, Please

Having said all that, however, the racial element, as compelling as it may be, is not essential to modern kidnap legends. Particularly in the light of recent events regarding child-kidnapping in South Africa, it is not surprising to find that both the victims and the villains are often transformed into ordinary, white, middle-class citizens, and the shopping malls are represented by respectable, even affluent, centres of commerce. This is the way one person remembered it:

When I first heard this I thought it was too strange to be true, but I've heard it a few times since then.

A woman was shopping at Sandton City with her son when she suddenly realised he wasn't with her. She rushed to the security people and they quickly closed off all the exits.

They searched everywhere and eventually found the child in the toilets with a young couple. His hair had been cut and dyed, his clothes changed, and he had been drugged.

They were apparently going to use him for porno movies.

The story has a frightening ring of truth, coming at a time when child molestors, paedophilia, sex rings and child kidnapping have become a shocking reality in the headlines

44

and front pages of our newspapers.

A more detailed version of the story came from a correspondent who placed it firmly in this context. He wrote that it 'related to the recent shocking kidnappings of young girls... the story was told as if it had actually happened in Kempton Park, Menlo Park, Cresta and Durban North':

> *A mother of two was shopping with her children and realised that she had taken two cans of jam when she only needed one. She picked up the extra one and sent her daughter, a four-year-old blonde, back up the far end of the aisle to replace the jam.*
>
> *Before turning into the next aisle she looked back to see where her daughter was and the child was not in the aisle. She rushed down to the end where she had sent the child and could not see her in either the aisle to the left or the one to the right.*
>
> *Luckily she ran to the store manager and demanded that he close the shop, which he did, and several people began searching for the girl.*
>
> *It could only have been 10 or 15 minutes later when they found her in one of the toilets, with her head shaved, and she was almost asleep, having been drugged, as the doctor later found.*

People have told me that they recall hearing versions of the story in which the kidnappers are so experienced that they are able to grab children in an aisle, drug them, change their clothes and dye their hair on the move, as it were, in the time it takes the mother to move from one aisle to the next. Before anyone can react, the child is long gone, and no one even sees it happen.

In the American versions, however, this variation usually ends with the mother or a store official catching the abductors in the act and rescuing the child.

This legend seldom seems to develop racial overtones, and relates more immediately to the fears of raising a child in an unstable society. While the sex, drugs and pornography elements are frightening in themselves, they are also not essential to the legend. In some versions, the kidnapping is related to illegal adoption rackets.

The couple who carry out the kidnapping has been said, by folklorists, to be a metaphor for the breakdown of the nuclear family and the social confusion this causes. However, there are simpler ways of understanding the legend.

The basic fear being played on is first and foremost the loss of a child in a situation where this could have been prevented by vigilance. It is therefore a warning to mothers to exercise proper control and care over their children, and not to neglect their 'natural' function as protector and nurturer of children. Where they fail in that role, they will be punished by having their children removed from them: predators of the most vicious nature are ready to pounce.

And that brings us to one of the most tragic tales of child kidnapping to emerge from the headlines in recent years: the apparent kidnapping, imprisonment and disappearance of five young girls by a known paedophile who committed suicide as police closed in on him, without the fate of the children having been revealed. A sixth girl, who has not been linked to the paedophile, is usually included in the reports and discussions of the case. All disappeared between August 1988 and November 1989. There has still been no firm evidence of their fate.

So what is their connection with urban legends? After all, these are true and genuinely tragic cases. The answer lies in an unusual reversal of the urban legend process. In this case, elements of the urban legend have intruded into the reality of an intensively investigated crime.

On 18 June 1989 the *Sunday Times* 'revealed' a possible link between the disappearance earlier that month of one of the girls to a ring of pornographic movie-makers.

On 21 October 1989 the *Saturday Star* reported that the parents of the girls believed they had been smuggled out of the country. Police had followed up this suggestion and had made enquiries 'overseas', but these had come to nothing. The father of one of the girls told the *Saturday Star* that he had made contact with the 'underworld', and had been told that a syndicate was operating in all major cities.

'They are running a prostitution and sex racket involving youngsters,' he told the newspaper.

The first conscious mention of urban legends came on 3 December 1989, in a *Sunday Times* report by Terry van der Walt. She wrote, among other things, that 'Mr Harvey and his wife are certain their daughter was abducted but they have reconsidered their initial fears that she may have fallen prey to a child sex ring.

'Urban legends about girls being abducted and taken out of the country as sex slaves appear too far-fetched for Mr Harvey to believe.'

On 27 December 1989 the *Citizen* reported that police spokesman Brigadier Chris Serfontein had rejected the possibility of white slave traders as well as pornographic rings being responsible for the abductions.

'The girls have been gone for so long with no indication as to their whereabouts that police have had to examine all the possibilities,' he told the newspaper. 'Although anything is possible, police have absolutely no indication whatsoever that white slave traders may have kidnapped the girls.'

And then, on 11 January 1990, Cornelius 'Gert' van Rooyen and his accomplice, Francina 'Joey' Haarhoff, abducted a 16-year-old girl who escaped, and eventually led police to the house, where five of the missing girls had apparently been kept at one time or another.

In the ensuing chase, Van Rooyen shot Haarhoff and himself in an apparent suicide pact.

Subsequently, unconfirmed reports have cropped up

from time to time, placing one or other of the girls in various locations across the country. Some of these suggest that the girls may have become part of a child sex ring, whose members keep the girls hidden away.

In the light of highly publicised police crackdowns on child sex rings in Johannesburg, Cape Town and Durban, this speculation has a ring of truth. However, it is too close to urban legend territory for comfort.

Whether the mystery is solved or not, it has made a dramatic impact on the attitudes of parents towards the security of their children. More effectively than any cautionary tale or urban legend, the reality will have driven itself deeply into every parent's consciousness. Does this mean the related urban legends will no longer have a function?

If anything, the events will probably give the legends an added sense of immediacy, urgency and significance.

The solid weight of regular police statements and newspaper reports will overwhelm any amount of proof that some of these reports are merely urban legends that are told around the world.

Footnote

A bizarre story emerged almost immediately in the wake of Van Rooyen's death.

I have heard from several third-hand sources that, during the course of 1989, advertisements appeared in the classified columns of Pretoria newspapers offering antique furniture for sale. Prospective buyers would arrive at an address given over the phone, which turned out to be the home of Gert van Rooyen.

Of course, his name meant nothing at the time. When they asked to see the antiques, he pointed out cheap, functional items of furniture of very recent vintage, such as trestle tables and stack-chairs. The customers were not amused, and asked to see the real antiques.

He insisted these were the ones: 'If you hold onto it for fifty years,' he said, 'it will become an antique.'

Urban legend? Almost certainly. But why Van Rooyen? Why antiques? Perhaps the story arose because of the need to switch off from the horror of what Van Rooyen represented. It is funny and it deals with a criminal aspect of Van Rooyen which does not necessarily give parents sleepless nights. It presents Van Rooyen as a petty crook, which is a much easier concept to cope with, subconsciously, than the sex monster portrayed in the media.

6

OF HEARSES AND CURSES

International urban legends about kidnapping provide South Africans with a rich vein of subconscious fears. But what of the entirely indigenous kidnap tales? Do they serve similar functions? Are they independent of, yet in the same tradition as the international urban legend mainstream?

To explore these questions, I have pursued several powerful South African urban legends. They all include elements of tragic, verifiable reality.

Legends in the Forest

In 1969 a young student of the University of Cape Town, Rosalind Balinghurst, went camping in the Knysna forest with some friends. During their stay, she hitch-hiked to the nearby town of George to buy supplies. She was never seen again.

That was the factual, reported event.

There were many rumours at the time: she had been kidnapped by a cult that lived deep in the heart of the forest. They had drugged her and forced her to join them, or they had murdered her.

The story was used as a warning to young women throughout the 1970s: stay away from the Knysna forest. Do not hitch-hike.

Before examining the Balinghurst legend in more detail, it would help to consider the atmosphere of the Knysna forest, and the earlier legends associated with it.

The forest was once the home of large herds of elephant, but indiscriminate hunting killed them off to the extent that only a handful remain, living in remote parts of the forest. An Automobile Association travel guide, *Off the Beaten Track*, tells this brief story of an elephant hunter:

> *(A) renowned hunter by the name of Marais is said to have accounted for exactly 99 animals. He boasted that before killing his hundredth he would first pluck a hair from its tail. He did indeed pluck the hair, but No 100 succeeded in killing him in the process.*

Then there is the legend of George Rex of Knysna. This British settler arrived in the area in 1804 and worked hard to develop Knysna as a port. His boat, the 127-ton *Knysna*, regularly traded off the coast. However, in those days already, there were dark rumours that George was the illegitimate son of King George III of England, sent to South Africa to prevent scandal. His very name, which was obviously Latin for King George, was all the evidence most people needed. But the story was never proved or disproved, and the legend persists to this day.

The Knysna forest has been the setting of several novels, including Dalene Matthee's *Circles in the Forest* and *Fiela's Child*, both of which have been made into successful films.

It is a refuge not only for a dwindling population of elephants, but also for an isolated community of people who live according to their own rules and rituals, cut off from the outside world, and marrying among each other for generations, much like the popular cinema image of the hillbillies in America's Cajun country.

Author Wessel Ebersohn moved from the bustle of Johannesburg to an isolated hut in the Knysna forest in the late 1980s so that he could concentrate on his writing. He has evocatively captured the nature of the forest and its people in an essay entitled 'The People of the Forest', published in the Autumn 1990 edition of *Excellence* magazine:

51

> *In a place like Soetkraal, a hamlet at the bottom of a valley in the Outeniquas (a mountain range near Knysna) that has never been connected to the world by more than a sled path, perhaps a dozen families lived with little outside contribution to the community gene pool for almost 100 years ... Some were blind, others had grotesquely twisted limbs. Many had strange lumps on their bodies and many could not learn.*

But the isolation goes deeper, says Ebersohn:

> *The ever-present screen of trees limits not only physical vision, but the extent to which the mind can reach as well.*
> *The world beyond the forest's limits is so wide and unprotected, its people so strange and forbidding, that life out there is all but unthinkable.*

If that's what it's like to insiders looking out, it applies doubly to outsiders looking in. Here is a world of unreal beauty and strange terrors. And into this world, one day in 1969, walked Rosalind Balinghurst.

The Ritual of Repentance

The original event — the disappearance of a girl in the Knysna forest — was fertile soil for the growth of an urban legend and gradually, the rumours did begin to crystallise into legend. My first encounters with it were so vague, I was inclined to dismiss it as a mere rumour, but friends insisted I follow it up, and finally I was rewarded with two similar stories that were pure urban legend. The first example was told to me like this:

A few years ago an acquaintance of a friend of mine committed some minor crime and spent some time in gaol.

While he was there, he met a highly-strung Coloured guy.

On a certain day of the year, this guy would get real tense, and then he would go through a strange ritual. He would pray and meditate all day long, insisting that he had to repent. This was his repentance ritual.

The other guy kept asking him what it was all about, and finally he confessed, privately, that he had participated in a murder many years before. He had been part of a group of satanists, who had had a coven in the Knysna forest. One night they had decided to sacrifice someone.

For some reason, they were sure someone would come along. Meanwhile, said this guy, Rosalind Balinghurst had gone for a walk in the forest, and come upon the coven. They grabbed her and sacrificed her in a satanic ritual.

Afterwards, he felt such remorse, he went through this same repentance ritual every year on the anniversary of the murder.

The style of the story is peculiar to urban legends. It includes several perennial motifs or symbols folklorists use to classify urban legends. There is the tragedy that is recalled on its anniversary; the apparently supernatural mystery that is finally explained; the strange ritual, and the eventual confession; the remorse of the guilty party; and the apparent punishment — ending up in gaol — for apparently unrelated crimes.

The legend seems to have several clear intentions: one is specifically and simply to explain a great mystery. A second is the traditional cautionary tale function: it gives mothers ammunition to persuade their daughters not to hitch-hike, and to stay away from forests.

A third intention (explored more fully in the next chapter) relates to the perils of meddling with the occult.

A second version of the Knysna legend is even more typical of urban legend structure, as it involves a subsequent attempt to verify what is only suspected early in the story.

As before, it begins with an acquaintance meeting a man in gaol, and observing a repentance ritual ...

... the bloke finally confesses that he had once got stoned in the Knysna forest with a bunch of people who were pretending to be satanists. They were all taking drugs, and then they had a wild orgy.

Suddenly this girl appeared in the clearing. They thought she was an apparition, so they attacked and killed her. When they woke up the next morning, they saw a dead girl lying there.

They were so shocked, they buried her body and split up.

Every year after that, on the anniversary of the murder, this man felt so conscience-stricken, he had to go through a ritual of repentance.

Anyway, the chap who heard this story in prison eventually gets out and, going on the slim details he has heard, and the date each year that the ritual takes place, he discovers that only one victim fits the facts: Rosalind Balinghurst.

Talk about a multi-layered legend. There is no mention of why the murderer is in gaol, but it is abundantly clear that he is being made to suffer for his past crime. He must spend the rest of his days repenting — beside the fact that he languishes in gaol, seemingly, to this day.

There is also that double warning against dabbling in satanism and in drugs. As far as urban legends are concerned, playing with the occult — as the next chapter will show — bears the same consequences as being a fully fledged Satan worshipper. Even 'pretend' satanism results in death and misery. As for drugs, the only reward in urban legends can be death. It is perhaps superfluous to mention the cautionary element involved in a young woman going for a walk alone at night.

Finally, the legend has the classic 'detective yarn'

conclusion found in many crime legends. By putting two and two and two together, a great mystery is finally solved.

The Sinister Ambulance

While the Knysna legend began as a tragic event which acquired elements of rumour and finally developed into a full-blown urban legend, other legends have begun as pure rumour and finally led to tragic consequences.

Early in 1988, while I was working at the *Sunday Times*, a report reached us that a bogus ambulance had kidnapped children in the 'Coloured' suburb of Coronationville.

A few calls to the usual contacts turned up no formal charges, no complaints, no victims' names, and thus no story. The matter was dropped. But only at the newspaper.

In the townships, it was just beginning. A bogus hearse was added, and sightings were reported in neighbouring Ennerdale and Eldorado Park. Eventually, schoolchildren were said to have formed vigilante groups to protect themselves and their friends from the mystery abductors.

The story reached its first near-tragic climax when an ambulance — on legitimate business — was forced by a crowd to stop in one of the townships. The driver was dragged out and beaten. He was finally rescued by the police.

And then came this report in the *Star* on 10 March 1988:

> *Soweto police have disclosed that a five-year-old boy, abducted on his way from school in Molapo last Friday, was found inside a white minibus in which there were two coffins.*
>
> *A police spokesman said that despite widespread speculation about child abduction in Soweto, this was the only abduction case which had been reported to the police.*

55

The District Criminal Investigation Officer for Soweto, Colonel A Muller, said James Chabane of Molapo had earlier been abducted by three men travelling in a hearse.

He said the boy was with his aunt, Mrs Norina Chabane of Zola North, on a busy taxi route in Molapo when the hearse stopped next to them. The occupants of the hearse jumped out, grabbed the boy and drove away with him.

Colonel Muller said that later during the same day, at about 4pm, the boy's mother saw a mob running after a white minibus in Zola III.

She saw three men who were in the minibus – the driver and two passengers – being pulled out of the vehicle, stabbed with knives and set alight before their vehicle was also burnt.

The mob then opened and examined the two coffins in the vehicle and found there were corpses in them.

'While they were searching they heard a child screaming in the vehicle and when they looked further they found James hidden under the green undertakers' carpets,' Colonel Muller said.

He said the boy was unharmed.

Colonel Muller said the motive for the kidnapping was unknown to the police. However, the Soweto murder and robbery squad have detained a number of suspects for questioning in connection with the killing of five people accused of child abduction.

Could this have been an urban legend that turned out to be true? So it seemed, except that the trail ended as suddenly as it had been picked up. No further developments were reported by the press and suddenly the report began to sound a little suspect.

Consider this: the police account of the event was based

entirely on the evidence of one person who, by some amazing coincidence, happened to be the mother of the abducted child, snatched from her sister that morning. Then there is the tell-tale request from police for people to come forward with information.

The idea of a woman coming upon a mob attacking abductors, who turn out to have abducted her own child is so fantastic it sounds like something from the realms of cinema — or urban legend.

Then, just over a week later, on 19 March 1988, the *Citizen* carried this report:

CHILD-SNATCHING IS A RUMOUR SAYS SAP

Police are dismissing as rumour-mongering allegations that a bogus ambulance and a hearse are stealing children for muti in Black and Coloured townships on the Witwatersrand.

'Until such time as we have proof that children are disappearing and that an ambulance and a hearse are involved, we have no choice but to put down the allegations as rumours,' Lieutenant Pierre Louw, liaison officer for the Witwatersrand police, said yesterday.

Intensive investigations into the matter were launched after a 14-year-old Coloured girl claimed a minibus painted to resemble an ambulance, and a hearse, pulled up alongside her in Westbury two weeks ago.

She said the occupants had tried to abduct her. She later retracted her statement, saying she had made a false report because rumours of an ambulance and a hearse patrolling the township in search of children were circulating.

'These rumours have been rife in Soweto, Randfontein, Ennerdale, Eldorado Park and other townships for about a month, but police patrols in the townships

57

have found nothing to back them up yet,' Lieut Louw said.

'Furthermore, we have received no official reports of missing children.'

The public are nevertheless welcome to contact the police should they have concrete proof that children are going missing or that the two vehicles have been spotted.

However, Lieut Louw warned that making false statements under oath is an offence.

Luckily for folklorists, urban legends do not have to be repeated under oath. For them, one of the most fascinating aspects of this story would be that 14-year-old girl. In the report, she performs a classic role in the spread of urban legends, but one which is rarely documented so specifically: she has heard an urban legend as fact from someone else, and feels so strongly about it, perhaps even emotionally so, that she is willing to lie to police and claim it as a first-hand experience, just to give it the immediacy and credibility that, she hopes, will force the authorities to take action.

This is precisely the process we see at work in many media reports of urban legends — specifically in the case of the Oriental Plaza kidnappings and the ANC Homebuyer story.

This legend, despite originating in a politically oppressed community, is partly of the racial intolerance variety. Superficially, it relates to the same fears of abduction by mystery kidnappers as those we find in international abduction legends. It is a cautionary tale, told by parents to children as well as by children to their peers, and it is an immediate descendant of the old injunction to children: 'Never climb into strangers' cars.'

One word in the report, however, reveals the darker intent of the legend: the children are being stolen for 'muti' — substances used by traditional healers, sangomas and inyangas, to perform magical deeds. Supposedly, human flesh provides the most powerful muti.

The Muti Baby

The implications of muti in this kind of legend can be more
effectively examined by reference to another 'new' urban
legend. The first oral version I heard, during mid-1990,
went like this:

I don't know if this is true, but I heard it from a friend whose
mother says her maid told her. Anyway, her mother believes
it. Her mother's maid has been told, apparently, that the
price for young white boys for muti in the Pietermaritzburg
area has increased from R400 to R40 000. Although no boy
has been taken, the search is on. It's apparently happening
now, in Maritzburg. So everyone in Maritzburg is scared
and they're watching their kids, especially ones under about
the age of seven.

The rumour was rife, and then this report appeared in the
Sunday Times on 3 June 1990:

WITCH-DOCTOR HUNTS WHITE CHILD FOR HIS PEACE MUTI

*Terrified parents are keeping a close watch on their
children following a bizarre offer by a witch-doctor to
pay R10 000 for a white child to use for muti.*

*The witch-doctor said he would use the child to brew
up muti to end the violence in Natal, but a concerned
parent has offered a R10 000 reward for anyone who can
put the evil Maritzburg muti-man behind bars.*

*Police first became aware of the witch-doctor's
intentions last month when a distraught domestic worker
told her employer a man had offered her R2 000 for the
two-year-old child she was looking after.*

*When the woman refused to hand over the boy to the
witch-doctor, he repeated his offer to the next-door*

59

neighbour's maid who had come outside to investigate the commotion.

She was accompanied by her own young child as well as her employer's two toddlers. The maid, in tears, refused, saying she was a good Christian and could not give the man an innocent child.

The two maids barricaded themselves inside the homes and telephoned their employers, saying a man had tried to 'buy' the children. The police were alerted but no arrests were made.

And this week the witch-doctor tried again through two middlemen, but this time the offer was upped to R10 000. He was thwarted again, but fears are growing that if he persists he will eventually succeed.

Police liaison officer Lt Henry Budhram said the smartly dressed middlemen knocked on the door of a house in the suburb of Montrose and asked the maid if there were any young children living in the house.

Speaking in halting Zulu, they told the maid her employers' three-year-old son was needed for muti to stop the unrest. The maid managed to slam the door in their faces and immediately reported the incident to her employer. Police have opened two attempted kidnapping documents.

... The domestic workers approached by the witch-doctor said they had immediately known what he was because he wore a costume, complete with horns on his head and animal skins wrapped round his body.

From a journalistic point of view, the report has several problems: no names of intended victims; none of the maids quoted directly; the bizarre and unlikely garb of the 'witch-doctor' in the middle of suburbia, particularly in the light of the middlemen dressed in the opposite extreme of suburban formality; the brazen approach to domestic workers who clearly are horrified by the idea and would set the police on these people if they saw them again: none of this is questioned by the reporter.

On these grounds, it seems fair to assume the report is based largely on hearsay.

From an urban legend point of view, the story is riddled with powerful symbols, almost archetypes: there is the 'evil muti-man', the 'good Christian', the 'innocent child', the overt fear and the hidden warning that the muti-man will eventually succeed.

As in many urban legends in which the reliability of eye-witnesses may be questionable, the report uses the 'validating' technique, ie quoting authority figures who do not necessarily confirm the report, but whose mere presence in the report lend it credibility. Beside the police officer, the reporter also interviewed an academic:

> *A lecturer in social anthropology at the University of Natal, Durban, Mr Jeremy Evans, said human flesh was especially prized by witch-doctors as it was believed to make powerful muti.*
>
> *'There is a general basic belief that human flesh is powerful. We can only speculate as to why he wanted a white child, because in most instances of muti-murders the witch-doctor has sought out as dark a child as possible.*
>
> *'Children and old people are usually the victims of ritual murders because they are the most vulnerable and accessible.'*
>
> *... Mr Evans said it was unusual for a sangoma to seek out his victims himself. 'What usually happens is a client asks a witch-doctor to help achieve a specific goal. The witch-doctor then decides what medicine is necessary and gives the client a list of the ingredients for that medicine.*
>
> *'The dirty work is usually done by middlemen, particularly if the client is someone rich and powerful. In*

61

this case it appears the client is wealthy because of the huge reward he is offering.'

Despite the air of authority that Evans' presence lends the story, he unintentionally points a finger at several aspects that dent its credibility: the intended victim seemed inappropriate; the manner of the original approach seemed inappropriate.

The most damning element of all, of course, is the lack of witnesses' names. Not so the next edition of the saga. The *Star* carried this report on the front page of its issue of 29 June 1990, along with a colour photograph of the domestic worker and the child:

MAN TRIES TO BUY BABY FOR WITCH-DOCTOR

Two men tried to buy a 14-month-old baby for a witch-doctor, a young Roodepoort mother told the Star *yesterday.*

Debbie van Ryneveld, of Witpoortjie, said she was shocked when her maid, Mina Thabedi, telephoned her at work and told her that two men had offered R1 000 for her son Chandre.

When Mina refused to hand over the baby, the men said they would send someone later with R5 000 to collect it for a witch-doctor.

Mrs van Ryneveld and her husband rushed home immediately and telephoned the police.

The police kept a watch on the house from a side street, Mrs van Ryneveld said. At about 3pm a man shouted to the maid from across the road that he had come to collect the baby.

But then he realised the parents were at home and said he would be back today.

Mrs van Ryneveld said her husband would be able to

62

> identify the man, but the police did not see the incident.
> Since the ordeal she has taken Chandre and Mina to
> work with her. 'I am too scared to leave my baby at
> home,' she said.

Interestingly enough, that last line echoes almost precisely
what mothers in Maritzburg were apparently telling their
friends during this period.

Once again, the only true witness to the Roodepoort
event, the domestic worker, is not directly quoted. The
police presence is attested to by only one witness, whose
behaviour is precisely in accordance with what urban
legends would demand of her.

The reporter has not asked for police comment, as is
usual journalistic practice, so there is no formal, first-hand
confirmation that the police were at the scene. And if they
were, the men in question should consider a different
profession: they went to stake out the scene of a potential
crime and did not even notice the attempt being made. As
for the muti-man, he must have been seriously deranged to
shout out for all the neighbourhood (except the police) to
hear that he had 'come to collect the baby'.

Now the report may well be true. There is no reason for
anyone to make up such stories — except that it would
make a perfect urban legend.

First, baby threatened with a hideous fate while mother is
away at work; second, baby rescued in the nick of time; and
third, a veiled warning to other mothers.

The manner in which the legend emerged is strongly
reminiscent of the Oriental Plaza legend.

The first report, from Natal, is almost certainly an urban
legend. The second is probably not, although there are
elements in favour thereof. Let us assume it is a true story.
What then of the earlier report? What does it mean?

The report, and the ones about ambulance and hearse
abductions, have a ring of truth because of the very real, and

63

bloody, trail of 'muti murders' in South Africa. There have been several court cases in which sangomas and inyangas, as Southern African witch-doctors are properly known, have been charged with abducting, murdering and mutilating their victims. In some cases, middlemen have been arrested for these acts.

However, the manner in which the two muti baby stories — particularly the 'peace muti' version — emerged, seems to suggest that a similar process is under way as was the case in the Oriental Plaza legend (when a woman claimed her friend had been kidnapped, clearly having only heard rumours of such events) and the Sinister Ambulance episode in which a young girl heard a rumour and then claimed it as her own experience in order to get authorities to take it seriously.

Stories about muti have a significant place in black oral tradition. They seldom emerge in white culture — oral or written.

A well-known exception is a Nadine Gordimer short story — which may well have its origin in a township urban legend — entitled 'The Suitcase'.

Briefly, a man spots an unattended suitcase on a bus travelling to Soweto. When it becomes clear that its owner has long since disembarked, he surreptitiously claims it for himself. After alighting from the bus, he is stopped by police, who ask him what he has in the suitcase. 'Clothes,' he says, taking a wild guess. Of course, they open the suitcase and find it filled with human body parts — destined for muti. While the story is told by a white writer, it remains embedded in black experience.

The 'muti baby' legend — or report — is a rare crossover, involving both the white and black communities. It serves the urban legend cause well from several points of view.

It comes at a time of increasing integration, more freedom for blacks, and more uncertainty for whites. To ultra-conservative minds, integration represents a breakdown of cultural barriers, and ultimate destruction of their own culture.

The 'muti baby' symbolises these fears in the most crude and vicious manner. Muti, to many whites, represents all that is supposedly evil about black culture. White babies, on the other hand, represent the future of the white race. Sacrificing the baby for muti has a subconscious parallel with sacrificing the future of the white race to black culture.

The added element, in the Natal report, of the innocent baby's death bringing peace to Natal, is practically a Messianic touch, with the implication of sacrificing a sinless son for the sake of the survival of a community.

However, the Natal violence is largely confined to black political rivalry, so that to the white paranoiac it becomes, again, a matter of sacrificing the white future for the survival of the black race.

The legend is not necessarily racist in itself. It would be a shocking enough story to anyone — no matter what their race. It would bear repeating on its own merits or demerits.

Nevertheless, the psychological underpinning is a clear indication of the level of uncertainty and suspicion that stands between apartheid and democracy.

The Zombie Pop Star

No such political conclusions or extrapolations can be drawn from the most compelling muti legend of recent times. South Africa's own version of the 'Elvis is Alive' myth has been playing itself out over the past five years.

Here is the legend:

Paul Ndlovu, lead singer of the township pop group Mordillo, who was officially buried on 27 September 1986 after being supposedly killed in a car crash, had actually been kidnapped by an inyanga. Using powerful muti, she had turned Paul into a zombie — one of the living dead — and was using him as a slave. Several people had seen Paul at the inyanga's home, and he had been spotted all over the Transvaal by people who had known him.

And here, apparently, are the facts, as relayed by Ike Motsapi, a friend of Ndlovu's while he was alive, and a journalist for *Bona* magazine. He reported his findings in the magazine's July 1989 edition.

I HAVE SEEN PAUL – ALIVE!

It was a story like no other – a man who I had known well, whose death I had mourned, had been reported to be alive – 3 YEARS after he had been reportedly killed in a car crash on his way to another music engagement. It was fantastic.

So I began investigating, but it was not to be an easy search.

For weeks I chased the facts all over the northern and eastern Transvaal as well as the PWV area. Meetings that had been arranged never materialised ... People who were to give me facts never gave them ...

At last, however, the trip I had been longing for finally got under way – I was on my way to see whether the rumours really were true ... That Paul Ndlovu was alive.

We, that's photographer Dumi Ndlovu (no relation to Paul), driver Alex Sithole and myself left Johannesburg for the far northern Transvaal, where Paul was reportedly being treated by an inyanga. Paul's mother, Mrs Kate Ndlovu, had told us herself that she made a trip once a month to see her son and to pay the inyanga R100 for Paul's board and lodging while undergoing treatment.

The area in which Paul was supposed to be was near the town of Bochum, close to the Botswana border. First,

*however, we had to travel to Phalaborwa to collect Mrs
Ndlovu. The next morning, after spending the night in
Paul Ndlovu's house at Lulekani, Phalaborwa, we set out
for the northern Transvaal.*

*Later, after a long and tiring drive, we arrived at a
heavily guarded kraal which Paul's mother entered first,
to introduce us to the people within. Later she came to
call us – but before entering the kraal we had to remove
our shoes and discard any articles – including our
cameras.*

Only then were we allowed to enter.

*We were first introduced to a woman who I learned
later was the inyanga who was treating Paul. Her name
was given as Mapoulo.*

*Then we were asked to pay R200 if we wanted to see
Paul. Of course, we paid the R100 each – seeing Paul was
the whole point of the trip.*

*Then, while we waited for Paul to be brought to us,
Mapoulo told Mrs Ndlovu that seven days previously,
that is on April 19, there had been an attempt to kidnap
Paul from the kraal. According to Mapoulo, people in a
minibus with false number plates confronted Paul and
told him that they had been sent by Mrs Ndlovu to take
him home. They tried to force Paul into the minibus,
Mapoulo said, but Paul resisted, saying that he had to
fetch his clothes. Then he ran to the nearest police station
to seek help.*

*According to Mapoulo, some policemen from
Dendron chased the would-be kidnappers but could not
apprehend them and later discovered that the vehicle's
number plates were false.*

*Mapoulo then strongly urged Mrs Ndlovu to relax
because her son would be released into her custody soon
– on May 6.*

*Then came the moment we had been waiting for:
Mapoulo suddenly flung out her arm and pointed to a*

spot not far from where we had been sitting.

Paul Ndlovu stood there!

I could not believe my eyes, but I at last managed to raise my arm and wave to him.

He waved back, but I was not allowed to go closer to him – we were about 9 metres apart – and after a few moments, he was ushered away. For a while I stood dazed, then I recovered my senses. My thoughts went back to my memories of Paul and I was soon sure that whatever I had thought to be true – that Paul was dead – had been turned upside-down.

The man I saw was the Paul Ndlovu I had thought was dead, killed in a road accident three years ago!

No matter how I tried, however, I was not allowed to meet Paul and find out what had happened and so we returned to Phalaborwa where Mrs Ndlovu told us how she had been helped by Mapoulo to 'bring my son back to me'.

This is her story:

Three years ago, on September 16, 1986, Mrs Ndlovu was told that her son had been killed in a road accident at Natalspruit. Paul died as a result of being slammed against an electricity pylon – he was certified dead on arrival at the Natalspruit hospital.

'Immediately, Paul's late father and I drove from Phalaborwa to Tembisa (said Mrs Ndlovu) where we planned to stay while trying to find out what happened and also to arrange the funeral. We went to the Natalspruit police station to see the policeman who had sent for the ambulance in which Paul had been taken to hospital, but we were told the policeman was not on duty. We tried to establish his identity as well but so far we've neither met him nor found out who he is.

'We also wanted to see the vehicle but when we asked what had happened to it, the policemen didn't know. Eventually, after a two-day search, we found it at a

scrapyard at Alberton,' said Mrs Ndlovu.

'However, the scrapyard owner couldn't explain to us how the vehicle got to his yard!' she added.

Mrs Ndlovu then told us that when she and her late husband went to identify the body at the mortuary she doubted whether the body she saw really was Paul. But, as she puts it, she accepted that Paul was dead.

However, two things that put doubts in her mind were the fact that Paul's clothing was bloodsoaked, but also had sand on it – despite the fact that he had been pulled from the vehicle. And not all his possessions were present: his wristwatch, armbelt, cap, bracelet and left shoe were missing.

Mrs Ndlovu was also troubled by the report of the person seen running from the scene of the accident. She wondered why this person did not come forward and tell the family what had happened.

'All these things left too many questions unanswered,' she said...

A few days before the funeral ... Mrs Ndlovu's sister told her that there were two people who had come to see her. They wanted to talk about Paul.

'It was a man and woman. They had apparently taken their child to an inyanga in Tembisa for treatment but were shocked when they saw Paul's missing belongings in the inyanga's "surgery" with a photograph of Paul next to them. They told me that the inyanga was patronised by a person in show business...

'Then they begged me to do something because they suspected witchcraft,' said Mrs Ndlovu.

That's when Mrs Ndlovu first went to see Mapoulo, who told her that her son was being held captive by another inyanga but that she (Mapoulo) had the power to bring him back. So Mrs Ndlovu paid the required fee and returned to Tembisa to tell the family what had happened. But she did not know whether to believe Paul was alive or dead, though Mapoulo had told her to return after a week to see her son.

'Funeral arrangements were finalised and Paul was to be buried on September 27, 1986, at Phalaborwa... Then, during the day of the funeral, family members and people who knew Paul told us we were burying the wrong person!' said Mrs Ndlovu...

A week after the funeral, Mrs Ndlovu went to see Mapoulo. Here, in her own words, is the story of that visit:

'I could not believe my eyes when I saw Paul. I went to touch him to make sure he was alive. He hugged me and recognised me and it was a great day for me because I knew it was him,' she told me. Since that visit, she says she has been visiting Paul once a month, every month. But she is still not completely happy about all that has happened:

'What puzzles me is why and how these people managed to "declare" Paul dead when he was alive. I still want to know how they did it.'

That's assuming he IS alive. But there are many people who dismiss the whole story as absolute rubbish, or as a big, bad joke! It seems that more than one showbusiness personality has been accused at one time or another of being behind Paul's death but personalities we spoke to dismissed all the accusations as nonsense. They said the courts are there to deal with such matters...

We also telephoned the Bochum police, who are responsible for the Madikana area in which Paul is said to be undergoing treatment. Warrant Officer Moses Seanego dismissed the rumours of Paul being alive as rubbish.

'We have heard the rumours here and I can tell you this is all absolute nonsense!' he said. He added that no policemen from his station were ever involved with an

70

alive Paul Ndlovu and they had never been called out to protect him from any kidnap action, and anyway, they would not believe such nonsense.

'There is no Paul Ndlovu in our area,' says Warrant Officer Seanego.

So – is Paul alive, and if so when will we all be able to see and touch him and talk to him about his experiences? Or is he dead, as we all thought he was, and is all this nonsense ... a big, bad joke? I am convinced the man I saw WAS Paul, but then I was NOT allowed to get closer. I was NOT allowed to talk to him. I was NOT allowed to touch him.

A footnote to the article records: 'Paul Ndlovu was due to be sent home to his mother on 6 May, when we would be allowed to talk to him, and to photograph him. Up to the time of printing this issue, however, he was apparently still not home. *Bona* will continue its investigations.'

In a conversation with Ike Motsapi in July 1990, he told me that, a year later, he had made no further progress. At one point, he had been assured the inyanga was about to release Paul to his mother, on which occasion there would be a traditional slaughtering and roasting of an ox. The press would be invited and they would finally be able to speak to Paul face to face.

However, according to Motsapi, a team of journalists from another publication went to the northern Transvaal to follow up the story, but did not follow the proper channels or protocol, and had deeply offended the inyanga, who had promptly cancelled Paul's 'return'.

Subsequently, reports had reached Motsapi that a record company executive had spotted Paul alive, behind the wheel of a delivery vehicle in the Johannesburg traffic. Another witness, a nurse who had known Paul, spotted him in Nelspruit in the eastern Transvaal. And his car had disappeared, without record, from the scrapyard where Ike had last seen it.

It is easy to see how traditional myth and superstition can evolve into urban legend. It is also easy to dismiss the role of muti and inyangas, since there is no objective evidence for their powers.

However, it should also be borne in mind that Africa's traditional medicine and healing practice is as little understood as the voodoo cults of the Caribbean, which until recently were unfailingly dismissed by Westerners as 'hocus-pocus'. New evidence has emerged, however, to suggest that there are powerful psychological and sociological forces at work in especially the Haitian voodoo culture.

White people's awareness of traditional medicine in South Africa is usually restricted to the word 'witch-doctor' — regarded by blacks as an offensive description of traditional healers. Generally, these 'witch-doctors' are viewed on the same level of stereotype as the voodoo priests of the West Indies. Muti legends where whites are involved therefore tend to present a simplistic, uninformed and judgemental view of traditional medicine.

But then, with the Paul Ndlovu legend as evidence, the same could perhaps be said of the black response.

Take the tale of ...

The Hand in the Fridge

There was a very successful businessman in Soweto a few years ago. He had come up from nowhere, and now it seemed he could do nothing wrong. He went from strength to strength in his business, scoring one financial coup after another. People couldn't understand how he could be so successful, and they began wondering about the secret of his success.

One day, a suspicious fellow went to the businessman's house to spy on him. Looking in through the kitchen window, he saw the man come into the kitchen, open the fridge, and start talking to it. He appeared to be asking questions, and seemed to be getting answers.

Next day, when the businessman was off at work, the spy broke into his house and went straight to the fridge. Inside, the businessman's gruesome secret was revealed: the severed hand of a white person.

Immediately realising its purpose, he asked it a string of questions. The hand stood up to answer 'Yes', and shook from side to side for 'No'. Of course, the spy turned thief and the hand was stolen. No one ever saw the thief in Soweto again.

The legend is told only in black circles, although it suggests various white prejudices. The very fact of a white person being mutilated for black gain would confirm white fears of supposed black 'barbarism'.

More subtly, the fact that white assistance — in the form of a frozen 'adviser' — is required to advance black interests, confirms the old-fashioned white attitude of paternalism towards blacks.

However, by the same token, this theme in the legend reflects crucial aspects of the black-white relationship fostered by apartheid over many years. On the one hand it suggests an inferiority complex engendered among blacks by this paternalism, Government enforced as it was. On the other hand, many blacks perceive whites as being wealthy — which, comparatively, most of them are, in the context of generally low black wages. The reason for white wealth, they sometimes assume, is because whites must be financial wizards: they know how to handle money. Having a white person, or even part of one, at your beck and call to advise you in business would thus give you a valuable advantage.

We can expect this kind of legend to fade away as black entrepreneurs are gradually allowed to compete with whites on an equal business footing.

The Stolen Voice

To put muti legends in a first-person, real-life context, here is the account of established entertainment figure Mazambane, an *mbaqanga* singer. He told journalist Ike Motsapi the following chilling story:

> *I narrowly missed being struck by lightning while I was performing at a concert, but I did lose my voice. I consulted a well-known inyanga in Swaziland, who told me there were people who wanted to turn me into a zombie. It was at the time when* mbaqanga *was very popular and I was a top singer. The inyanga said these people were particularly jealous of my voice. As treatment I had to spend five days in a dark hole dug in the ground, and was given no food or water. I did not see what was happening to me. I felt sleepy all the time. The person who had taken me to the inyanga kept vigil day and night because he thought I might die. When I was taken out of the hole I was surprised to discover that I had recovered my voice.*

As authentic as this account may be, it reflects a long-running theme in urban legends told in the township entertainment world.

As long ago as the 1950s, when township choir competitions were immensely popular and keenly contested, there was a fear of inyangas stealing star singers' voices. The Manhattan Brothers, a leading township group of the 1950s, were said to be on the alert for this kind of witchcraft all the time.

74

There was apparently enormous jealousy among rival choir stars, and every effort was made to 'psyche out' opponents. The ultimate method, of course, was to convince them that an inyanga had been hired to steal their voices.

Typically, a choir would arrive in the competition hall and a 'sympathetic' person would come up to the star singer and warn him that the other choir had a witch-doctor with them. If he sang that night, he would be sure to lose his voice for good. Usually, the terrified singer would pull out of the contest, and the other choir would win.

In some cases, the singer defied the warning, with great trepidation, and went up to perform. When he opened his mouth, all the time anticipating the worst, not a sound would come out.

It is reasonably certain that no witchcraft was involved — merely clever psychology, and highly suggestible victims — but that would have been cold comfort to the singers targeted by inyangas or rivals.

Ike Motsapi tracked down no less than three current music industry figures who claimed first-hand experience of 'stolen voices'.

William Mthethewa told this story:

A person who was sent to recruit me for another band told me I would regret not joining them. The following day I survived an attempt on my life. A powder-like substance was sprinkled on the door I would go through to my recording studio. But another artist went through the door first — and he died.

Then I went to Swaziland where I was contracted to perform in several shows. Someone involved in show-business bought me a cold-drink and gave it to me. I didn't suspect anything and drank it just before I was to go on stage to perform. When I got up to sing — my voice had gone. I tried to sing, but no sound came out of me.

I was rushed to hospital in Swaziland where I spent several months without recovering my voice. Then I was transferred to Baragwanath hospital (Soweto) and later went back to my home town, Welkom.

For two years I could not sing. Then I was introduced to a faith-healer who took me to some caves in Brandfort. After she performed some rituals she took me inside the caves where I heard the voices of people I seemed to know. These voices told me why I had lost my voice. Then I was given lots of water to drink and encouraged to vomit. I was shocked to see what came out of me, and surprised to find I had immediately recovered my voice.

Many people don't know that my comeback song, 'Mosamaria', which was a record-breaker, was dedicated to the faith-healer.

Fact? Fancy? The power of suggestion? These stories are, from a verification point of view, highly problematic, as there is no corroborating evidence. However, it is clear that the victims believe firmly in what appeared to have happened to them.

But then, that is not so unusual in the land of urban legends, as we shall discover in the next three chapters.

7 THE DEVIL MADE ME DO IT

While you do not have to be religious to believe legends about satanism, it does help. Satanism is perhaps one of the most controversial and emotive issues to be laid before the South African public in years.

The extent of media coverage it received in the middle of 1990 better reflected the fears of the public than the priorities of newspapers. Satanism grabbed the headlines, whether justified or not.

Its presence, for a while, at the top of news priorities, not to mention in urban legends, attests to the deep fear people harbour for the unknown. It goes beyond fear of spiders or of heights or foreigners. This is the ultimate unknown quantity, the consummate deadly but untouchable threat.

The very idea of demonic agents lying in wait to possess our loved ones — let alone ourselves — is terrifying to the believer, and at least deeply disturbing to the non-believer, or to believers in faiths which do not normally allow for demons.

After all, even if demons do not figure in our worldview, have we not seen proof of devilish rituals, bloody sacrifices and a range of assorted dark practices?

Upon closer investigation, it becomes clear that many of the claims about satanism have no basis in objective observation, and are entirely dependent on hearsay.

Hearsay ... or urban legend.

The most outrageous satanic legend yet to emerge in South Africa is the 'fact' that satanists are breeding babies for human sacrifice.

Several individuals, including prominent police officers, came forward during the first half of 1990 with 'proof' that sacrifices were taking place. The tales they reported were truly horrific, confirming anyone's worst fears about satanists in South Africa.

A kind of sub-legend, based on the fact that there is no law in South Africa prohibiting satanism *per se*, is that police are powerless to act against satanists, no matter how hideous their deeds.

Personality magazine, never one to restrain its investigative reporters, ran a cover feature on 14 May 1990, headlined 'I ATE A HUMAN HEART'.

The story begins:

> *I cooked and ate the heart of a Christian who had died, and in doing so believed I was cursing him and cursing God.*

The whole business, the article attested, started quite innocently:

> *It began with a game of 'glassy glassy' ... (but eventually) I became a full satanist after I attended a youth meeting in a Christian church. At that stage I was a drug addict. I tried everything on the market.*
>
> *A relationship with the minister's daughter followed, but the minister opposed it. So, with the aid of a 'priest of Satan', he put a curse on the congregation and the minister was eventually forced to move away and landed up in jail.*

Eventually this confessor 'attended all the ceremonies and the gatherings of the Order of Darkness', and the high priest took him to satanic services:

> *At such a ceremony, offerings were also brought – babies and people's organs, especially babies'. The heart, and even the kidneys. Where did the babies come from? There are many ways – if they aren't stolen, they are bought. I have never attended a baby sacrificing*

ceremony, but believe me, it does happen.

It does happen! Yet this self-confessed satanist had never seen it happen, despite attending 'all the ceremonies' of the Order.

Now the purpose of this discussion is not to heap ridicule on the individual concerned, or to try to expose him as dishonest or a charlatan. The man clearly believes what he says. The point is, the most horrific part of his claim is based on little more than hearsay.

Let us look at the claim about eating a human heart. The satanist told *Personality*:

> *Human organs? It wasn't necessary for us to steal them. They are easily obtainable ... The master of ceremonies distinctly said that this was the heart of a man who died in the name of God and we must eat the heart. We cooked it and ate it ...*

Perhaps they did eat something which may well have been a heart — human or animal — but it was on the word of a master of ceremonies, part of whose job would be to impress the gathering with the drama of the event, that they accepted it to be a *human* heart.

A week after this report, a satanist, presumably the same person, told the *Sunday Star* that the high priest who had originally taken him under his wing had been arrested and tried for armed robbery and attempted murder. He was currently serving a 25-year gaol sentence. Now his new high priest, said the satanist, had asked him to sacrifice his 4-year-old son to Satan.

In a footnote the reporter mentioned that Port Elizabeth police had set up the interview in an attempt to warn the public of the horror surrounding devil-worship.

On 4 June 1990, under a cover emblazoned with the headline 'SATANISM EXPOSÉ', the mystery satanist was revealed, along with photographs of his baptism, which took place on 19 May. It told a harrowing but inspiring tale of the man's conversion to Christianity.

This was followed by a report on Major Kobus Jonker, head of the Eastern Cape Murder and Robbery Unit, who had been interviewed in a reasonably balanced story in the 14 May *Personality* on his discovery of a satanist headquarters in East London. Jonker now told *Personality*'s Joey van Dyk that he had received death threats and warnings from satanists, but was not deterred.

Personality also referred to 'facts' revealed by Captain Leonard Solms, head of the Cape Peninsula's Child Protection Unit and anti-satanist crusader:

> *One of the most gruesome revelations was that at least 11 white babies have been killed and sacrificed in satanist rituals in the Cape in recent times.*
>
> *An unmarried mother, who took part in these rituals, said she bred a baby specially for sacrifice purposes. She said she was present when this child was killed.*
>
> *In Somerset West, satanist symbols were sprayed on the wall of an historic church. These included the mark of a high priest, which is usually displayed when a young virgin has been sacrificed and her remains have been buried in a Christian cemetery with the body of a cat or dog.*

The *Star* of 22 May 1990 had reported Captain Solms' allegation about the eleven babies specially bred for sacrifice. Solms' Child Protection Unit was inundated with calls from people offering information. However, a police liaison officer in Cape Town said that nothing 'concrete' had come to the fore. Evidence had been vague, and police in fact lacked any hard evidence at all. No bodies had been found, and no murder docket had been opened.

In a separate report on the same day, the *Star* spoke to several prominent religious leaders.

Occult expert Reverend Geoff Jamieson of the Presbyterian Church demanded that 'satanism be declared illegal ... These beliefs,' he said, 'destroy people.'

Nevertheless, despite his involvement in the field, he also had this to say on claims of child sacrifice, rape and sodomy: 'I know of these practices and that they take place — but I have never had anyone in South Africa report child sacrifice to me. Locally I have heard only of animal sacrifice.'

Bishop Wilfred Napier, president of the South African Catholic Bishops Conference, added: 'It is all hearsay.'

The Methodist Church's Reverend Jimmy Palos seemed to hit the nail on the head: 'There are already laws dealing with desecration and all other claims made. Where are the murder cases if police know these people eat hearts? There are laws against child sexual abuse mentioned with sacrifice rituals. Of course the church is totally against satanism, but one just wonders how many of these claims are substantiated. One wonders if this is some kind of ploy to evade real issues.'

The final word goes to the *Sunday Times*, which concisely expressed the attitude of more level-headed analysts in its Hogarth column on 27 May 1990:

> *That Cape police captain who recently provided hair-raising tales about devil-worship and human sacrifices should now be commanded by his superiors to produce something else – solid evidence and action.*
>
> *Devil worship may not be illegal, but the killing of babies most certainly is.*
>
> *And this policeman feels confident enough to talk of 11 children (some of them 'specially bred' for the purpose!) dying during rituals.*
>
> *If he knows enough to make such public announcements, he must know enough to pull people in for questioning.*

81

If he doesn't, his statements constitute reckless sensationalism and he should be carpeted.

There is a thin line between sensationalism and urban legend. We can be sure of seeing more unsubstantiated reports of babies being sacrificed. And we can probably be sure that no one will be brought to trial on related charges. For, as all the evidence seems to suggest, this is part of a series of urban legends that reflects South Africans' fear of the unknown.

To be perfectly frank, it may merely reflect fear — probably justified fear — of satanists and their dark practices. The symbolism of the occult threat, however, is a compelling metaphor for the paranoia of many South Africans where the future of this country is concerned.

This examination is not an attempt to deny the existence of satanism, but rather to put dramatic claims about the occult into a perspective of urban mythology and cautionary tales. The parallels to the muti stories, particularly the attempts to buy white babies for muti, are striking.

As Reverend Jamieson put it to the *Sunday Star* on 18 May 1990:

> *Many stories circulated on satanism and the occult are 'scare' stories, but it does not deny the fact satanism is practised in South Africa.*
>
> *A lot of evidence is often very circumstantial. It is almost always hearsay – this is what makes it so nebulous.*

8 LIVE SPELT BACKWARDS IS EVIL

In the land of urban legends, a special kind of hell seems to be reserved for youth culture. There are many people who have made idiots of themselves by believing everything they hear about satanism in rock music, but not many have been sued for trying to make others believe these things.

Dr Jannie Malan, a minister in the Dutch Reformed Church and moderator of its Southern Transvaal synod, falls into this latter category. He claimed that an album of alternative Afrikaans music, entitled *Voëlvry* ('free as a bird'), contained hidden satanic messages, and that it was designed to corrupt South Africa's youth.

Writing in the church mouthpiece, *Die Kerkbode*, on 7 July 1989, Malan accused the record's producers, Shifty Records, of using 'backmasking techniques' to convey 'devil-inspired messages' to listeners. He suggested that the records would be played backwards by impressionable youths, and the satanic messages so revealed would leave a deep impression.

Shifty challenged Malan to prove his allegations, or make defamation payment of R10 000. Malan insisted he could prove the allegations. On 21 September 1989 the two parties met with their respective lawyers and listened while the record was played backwards.

'But try as they might they could find no hidden "satanic messages" in the garbled cacophony,' reported *Sunday Times* writer Ivor Crews that weekend.

'As far as we were concerned it was totally unintelligible,' Shifty general manager Mark Bennett told the *Sunday Times*. Bennett said attacks on the album by 'various elements' of the church had adversely affected sales and

Shifty was now consulting lawyers. He added that the album had been banned on all Afrikaans campuses after the groups playing on it were accused of blasphemy and undermining the youth of the country.

On 3 October 1989, Shifty issued a statement that it had instructed its lawyers to issue summons against Malan.

'In the light of the influence wielded in certain circles by Dr Malan, and the seriousness of the allegations made in *Die Kerkbode*, we demanded proof of these allegations, or a retraction and an apology,' the statement ran. 'Dr Malan elected to prove his allegations.'

While this was not the first time teams of lawyers had been called in regarding backward masking, it was probably the first time that the accusers had been sued.

Backward masking, while it does exist, has proved to be one of the great urban legends of the music world. To be sure, there are several famous examples of backward masking, but also many equally legendary examples of people spotting backward masking where none existed.

In 1988, while editing a teenage magazine, I decided it was about time the myths were exposed, and commissioned Gus Silber, one of South Africa's leading exponents of pop-culture journalism, to write a feature on the issue. It was an hilarious but provocative and incisive look at the absurd claims made for backward masking.

The response from readers — and their parents — was astonishing. By mail and by phone, the vitriol poured in. Ironically, most of the abuse came from people who claimed to be deeply religious, although their language suggested otherwise. Nevertheless, because of the magazine's links with a major financial institution, it was almost closed down on the spot.

This is the claim which, in part, caused all the fuss:

The devil lives in the grooves of a Rock 'n Roll record. Because he is the devil, he wears a mask. When you play

*the record backwards, the mask slips off. You hear the
devil talking. You go crazy.*

*That's the theory, anyway, according to groups of
concerned parents and born-again evangelical cam-
paigners who claim rock 'n roll has ways and means of
turning you into a zombie slave of Satan. The theory is
called backward masking, and it has been a favourite
lobbying cry of anti-rock reactionaries ever since
America's Moral Majority discovered that the Devil had
the best music.*

*Rumours about a satanic conspiracy in the rock 'n
roll business have been rife for a long time, but it was
only in 1982 that an American Congressman, Robert K
Dornan, really set the rat among the pigeons. He
proposed a bill calling for all suspect records to be
labelled with the following warning: THIS RECORD
CONTAINS BACKWARD MASKING THAT MAKES
A VERBAL STATEMENT WHICH IS AUDIBLE
WHEN THIS RECORD IS PLAYED BACKWARD
AND WHICH MAY BE PERCEPTIBLE AT A
SUBLIMINAL LEVEL WHEN THIS RECORD IS
PLAYED FORWARD... **

*The way it is supposed to work is as follows: a Devil-
worshipping heavy metal group, for example, composes
a seemingly harmless lyric in such a way that it takes on
a new and sinister meaning when the record is played
backwards. That's the theory. But is it for real?*

*The answer is disappointing. Yes, there is a
conspiracy, but the conspiracy is against rock music
rather than against the forces of cosmic goodness. The
examples of satanically-inspired backward masking
cited by the zealots of the anti-rock brigade are either
ludicrously far-fetched, sheer phonetic coincidence or*

---

* The Arkansas State Senate passed a similar record-labelling bill in
February 1983 by 86 votes to 0.

sly baiting by rock bands who might enjoy a private laugh at some people's gullibility. To credit rock music with hidden demonic powers is vastly to overestimate its powers to change the world, let alone hearts and minds.

Several of the best-known examples are cited in the article. However, rather than prove that backward masking does not work, Silber set out to show that it does — but that many examples are rather innocuous. For instance, Pink Floyd, whose album *The Wall* was for a time banned in South Africa for its potential subversiveness (the track 'Another Brick in the Wall', which includes the line 'We don't need no education, we don't need no thought control', was used as a warcry by students boycotting 'Coloured' schools in 1982), included backward masking on one of the tracks. If you were to play 'Goodbye Blue Sky' backwards, you will hear the message: 'Congratulations. You have just discovered the secret message.'

Most messages, or alleged messages, however, are not quite as bland.

On 30 June 1989, the *Roodepoort Record*, a small regional newspaper, devoted two pages to a meeting held by the Roodepoort Assemblies of God church, where Andrew Grossman of Maranatha Christian Church had presented an illustrated talk entitled 'Rock and Roll — A Search for God'.

According to the *Record*, the presentation was developed by Reel to Real Ministries, USA, and is used throughout the world, incorporating a lecture, slides, music and lyrics.

The tone is set by highly selective quotes from Grossman, such as Aristotle's injunction that 'All music for the young should be regulated by law', and Lenin's theory that 'One quick way to destroy a society is through its music.' (And they didn't even have backward masking to contend with back then!)

Grossman devotes much of his talk to satanic symbols

used by various artists. There can be little argument with that — particularly as most of the artists cited have never bothered to unleash their lawyers.

However, when Grossman reaches the subject of backward masking, he falls into the old trap of repeating the *legends* about what the record reveals, rather than what the record actually reveals.

The main problem is that, if you listen hard enough, and have decided beforehand what you want to hear, or have been carefully prepared for what someone wants you to hear, then you are going to hear that message. In most cases, it is pure phonetic coincidence. However, as the *Record* reported, the following 'actual recordings of backward masking' were played at the presentation:

* 'Start to smoke marijuana', from Queen's 'Another One Bites the Dust'.
* 'He's the nasty one; Christ you're infernal', from Electric Light Orchestra's 'Eldorado'.
* 'You know Satan holds the keys to the lock', from Cheap Trick's 'Gonna Raise Hell'.
* 'Here's to my sweet Satan, no other made a path, for it makes me sad, whose power is Satan', from Led Zeppelin's 'Stairway to Heaven'.

While I was researching this subject I received a yellowed cutting, unfortunately not dated, from the Natal *Weekend Post*, which referred to a newspaper investigation of similar claims. Probably written in the mid-eighties, it tells of a decision by a California State legislature planning full-scale hearings on backward masking. The hearings were initiated by a politician who had been persuaded to do so by two 'experts', one a self-described 'neuroscientist' who had never graduated, and another a 20-year-old 'former rock music buff'.

The songs used as 'evidence' included ELO's 'Eldorado', along with songs by groups like Styx and Black Oak

Arkansas.

According to the report, a Johannesburg newspaper had launched its own investigation and had found no evidence for the claims, except for garbled tones which may have been interpreted any way a listener desired.

'Reporters listened to the ELO's "Eldorado" but the garbled tones failed to make their impact. Styx's local record company, RPM, played the master-tape of "Snowblind" backwards and the result ... was "backward-sounding music".'

Other objective investigators reported similar results, and one led to the ground-breaking study of conspiracies, trade secrets and popular myths, William Poundstone's *Big Secrets*. The chapter devoted to backward masking is probably the most exhaustive objective investigation yet made into the allegations.

For a rational response to these claims, it is essential to understand the mechanics of backward masking and reversed speech.

Says Poundstone:

> *Reversed messages are difficult to recover at home. Record turntables are not built to go backwards. Some have a neutral setting, in which the pickup and amplifier remain active and you can turn the record backwards by hand. But hardly anyone has a steady enough hand to produce satisfactory results...*
>
> *... Reversed speech has several unexpected features. One is that syllables are not a constant in the reversal process. A one-syllable word can have 2 or 3 syllables when played backwards. Thus (the words 'number nine') in the Beatles'* Revolution 9 *reverses to 'turn me on, Mr adman' – or something like it.*

Poundstone and his team hired a sophisticated studio, investigated the mechanics of backward masking and spent many hours listening to — or for — the subliminal messages allegedly contained in records. They examined all the best-known examples of supposed backward masking messages.

One example which is often bandied about in this country is 'Another One Bites The Dust', by the group Queen, which allegedly sends out the message: 'It's fun to smoke marijuana'.

Poundstone says, 'There is something that sounds like "It's fun to smoke marijuana" in the reversed music ... It might be rendered no less faithfully, however, as "sfun to scout mare wanna".

'Let's make a distinction between engineered and phonetic reversals. When an artist records a verbal statement, reverses it by turning the tape end to end, mixes the reversed statement into a master tape and has records and tapes produced from the master, that is an engineered reversal. When the phonetic properties of song lyrics are such that they can be reversed to sound like something else, that is a phonetic reversal.

'It's too easy to find coincidences. If, for instance, the letters of the alphabet are recorded in conventional fashion (Ay, Bee, Cee, etc) and reversed, several of them sound like English language words. D reverses to "eden", for example; F becomes "pray"; S becomes "say"; and V becomes "even".'

On 'He's the nasty one; Christ, you're infernal', attributed to 'Eldorado', Poundstone says, 'Coincidence ... Reversed, this passage becomes the expected hotchpotch of syllables — no one hearing it cold would describe it as anything but reversed music. Only if you listen while reading along with what you're supposed to hear will you get anything.'

In the Led Zeppelin song 'Stairway to Heaven', Poundstone says, 'Coincidence ... the Satan is good and clear, the rest isn't. The other alleged lines are unremarkable. All are phonetic reversals of the entirely lucid forward lyrics and obviously are just accidents.'

A new phase in the controversy opened up at the beginning of 1990. On 17 February the British magazine *New Musical Express* reported a campaign launched by top BBC disc jockey Chris Morris. His attention had been drawn to the supposed 'backward' message in Queen's 'Another One Bites the Dust' by a clergyman. This led him to check out current records on the BBC playlist, and he found them riddled with what he heard as subversive messages.

As an indication of the stretch of the imagination required to hear sinister messages, here is Morris in his own words:

> *You know at the end of the chorus on New Kids on the Block's 'Hanging Tough' where they go 'Ruff ruff ruff'? If you play that backwards it sounds like 'Hurry hurry hurry' – getting louder. And when they sing 'Hang tuff' – spin that backward and it sounds like 'I snigger' or possibly 'Ice Nigger'. This betrays the intelligence behind the hidden messages because it's a phonetic pun. 'Ice' is the new form of smokeable meta-amphetamine, and 'nigger' is clearly either a gratuitous racist insult or a code word for a dealer. Originally the 'Ice Nigger' was the black dealer who sold you the stuff on the block.*

According to Morris, the Carpenters' upbeat number 'On Top of the World' apparently includes this strange line: 'See that dog. Bite its head off. Ha Ha Ha.' This information, Morris claimed on the air, was given to him when the late Karen Carpenter came to him in a dream. He also claimed that teenybop acts like Jason Donovan and Kylie Minogue also dabbled in hidden messages.

Morris did not confine himself to the music itself, and decided to interpret band and artist names in his rather individual style as well. The 'Block' in the group New Kids on the Block is also slang, claimed Morris, for Beta-blockers, which ties into a hidden message on their record that says, 'Your days go whizzing when you're on heroin.'

Morris went further, disclosing that singer Madonna's name backwards was Annodam. And that Annodam was 'pig-Latin' for the 'Year of Damnation'. No doubt the Catholic Church would be interested to hear that one!

In October 1989, the aforementioned Dr Jannie Malan invited Rodney Seale, a 'so-called music expert', according to the Afrikaans-language morning newspaper *Beeld*, to address the Southern Transvaal Synod of the Dutch Reformed Church on backward masking. Seale apparently travelled around the country giving demonstrations with the aid of sound equipment, colour slides and record-players that played backwards as well as forwards. The intention of the demonstrations, reported *Beeld*, was to reveal that rock and pop music was sexually perverted and satanic. Included in the slide show was a still showing a scene of bestiality, which by implication was linked to rock music.

The presentation caused a storm of outrage among the conservative synod members — but not outrage aimed at rock music. Reverend Nelus Niemandt of the Weltevreden congregation stated that the generalisations and associations made during the presentation were offensive, and that it was dangerous to portray pop music as part of satanism. He proposed a motion that the synod make it clear that Seale did not represent its viewpoint. The Auckland Park congregation's Reverend Piet van der Merwe supported the resolution, and it was accepted 'with an overwhelming majority' — apparently by at least three-quarters of the 370 delegates.

Beeld's religious affairs reporter, Ina van der Linde, described Seale's presentation: 'Synod-goers sat glued to their seats for about an hour watching slides flash past them. Seale, like a well-practised charismatic preacher, told ... of the "four phases" through which rock music moves: sexual perversion, drugs, rebellion and satan-worship.'

Seale's bizarre claims included the 'fact' that research has shown that 79 per cent of teenagers who listen to rock music smoke marijuana and sniff a certain type of detergent.

'The slides varied from goats' heads in bowls of blood (which may have been soup), pop singers drinking blood, pop stars (including Boy George) dressed as women and made up, dead babies in a dustbin, dried out foetuses made into earrings and a man having sex with a pig.'

Although there was no mention of the connection of the latter with pop music, the message was clear, reported Van der Linde: 'Pop and rock music leads to all these things.'

The climax of the evening was intended to be Malan's clincher: Seale played selections from the *Voëlvry* album, and in particular a song called 'Slang' ('snake'), and repeatedly taped the chorus, which he then played backwards. He told the audience they would hear the words, 'Jesus name. God is nameless.'

Van der Linde reported that she could not hear it. While the synod vote did not prove or disprove anything, it was a major moral victory for the beleaguered pop industry, which is not to say that rock has regained the moral high ground. Far from it. Today, more than ever before, there are pop songs dealing explicitly, and often advocating, rape, incest and devil-worship. People who are opposed to pop music generally on moral grounds can find evidence enough for their views right there, on the surface, in open invitations to sin, as it were.

However, in the tradition of cautionary tales, it seems important for many of these people to find the sinister implications of the music hidden and almost unprovable — for that 'proves' just how diabolical the music really is.

What can be more sinister than messages that only the subconscious (or special sound equipment) can pick up?

92

What can be better designed to fan the flames of paranoia than secret messages designed to warp the thinking of the young?

The very existence of backward masking techniques makes the growth of this kind of urban legend inevitable. The fact that the technique is occasionally used for nefarious messages — whether tongue-in-cheek or not — gives an added spur to the urban legends about backward masking. Each real example makes the bogus examples more believable, compelling and absurd.

As this book goes into print, the first American court case involving backward masking has played itself out.

The band Judas Priest — itself a name for the anti-rock brigade to conjure with — was in the dock for 'causing' the death of two fans as a result of alleged backward masking messages on one of their records.

Associated Press reported on 15 July 1990 that Judge Jerry Carr Whitehead denied a defence motion to dismiss the case on grounds that the record was protected by the First Amendment, saying such protection existed for regular music and lyrics, but not 'secret hidden messages that the recipient does not know exist'. The judge stressed that he did not know whether such subliminal messages did indeed exist on *Stained Class*, the album in question. The lawsuit was proceeding as a products liability case, accusing the band and CBS Records of negligence and intentional and reckless misconduct.

Lawyers for Judas Priest argued that the two young men, James Vance, 20, and Raymond Belknap, 18, whose families were suing the band and their record company, committed suicide as a result of their troubled lives, rather than because of a song. Both had a history of drug and alcohol abuse, psychiatric disorders and physical abuse.

The lawyers denied that any subliminal message existed or that the band promoted Satan and suicide, as alleged by the boys' parents.

But what of the subliminal message? It was claimed that it could be heard subliminally on the track 'Beyond the Realms of Death', behind the lyrics, 'Yeah, I have left the world behind. I am safe now in my mind. I'm free to speak with my own mind. This is my life, this is my life, and I'll decide, not you.' Played backwards one was supposed to hear the words, 'Do it, do it'.

Satanism? Or perhaps more typical of the kind of sound that would result from a phonetic reversal?

However, on the evidence of *Big Secrets*, even if the words weren't there, if someone believed they were, they would hear them.

The Judas Priest case gave the legal community — and the world — an opportunity to observe at first hand the kind of company kept by the anti-music lobby in their backward masking claims.

Christopher Read, writing in the London *Guardian*, described a procession of 'expert' witnesses in the court in Reno, Nevada, who 'gave rambling accounts of a surreal world where subconscious symbols lurked on Ritz biscuits, and subliminal messages had the power to make warts disappear and to enlarge women's breasts':

> *Among the witnesses was a Las Vegas salesman who had produced the bust-boosting subliminal cassettes. He claimed that hidden messages on recorded material had supernatural powers, but his PhD credentials turned out to have come from a mail order firm specialising in doctorates. The judge dismissed his evidence.*
>
> *Out, too, went the theories of a probation officer who had published a handbook for schools and police forces in California on the dangers of heavy metal music and how to 'de-punk' fans. The manual contained warnings of the secret satanic meaning of the ban-the-bomb symbol (an upturned broken cross) and the sinister resemblance of the Jewish Star of David to the black*

magic pentacle.

The principal expert for the families of the two dead youths was Dr Wilson Key, the shaven-headed author of the best-selling paperback, Subliminal Seduction. *Almost everywhere he looks, Dr Key sees the word 'sex' and depictions of skulls and penises. He has observed one, or all three, in Ritz cheese crackers, Rembrandt paintings, and Abraham Lincoln's beard on the US five-dollar note. For him, the* Stained Class *album cover was a cornucopia of such devices.*

It is almost certain that this evidence against Judas Priest, rather than the group's own defence, persuaded the judge, on 24 August 1990, to rule in favour of the rock group.

In a 100-page judgment, Judge Jerry Whitehead said that the parents had lost because, as the *Guardian* reported the next day, 'they failed to prove the messages were intentional, and had been a cause of the suicides'.

More significantly, for urban legend country, he ruled that the words 'do it' that allegedly could be heard, were 'a chance combination of sounds'.

The message is: do not try putting urban legends in the dock ...

9   THE LADY VANISHES

Legends, tales of terror and ghost stories have always shared a close relationship. What town or city does not have at least one supposedly haunted house, and a variety of stories, or legends, to explain the haunting? Usually, such stories circulate among the local inhabitants, particularly adolescents, for whom haunted places have always had a curious fascination.

Among these are often stories that people grow up believing to be indigenous to their neighbourhood, only to discover, as they move away or come into contact with people from other towns or cities, that the same stories are claimed for numerous other locations.

When this happens you are probably no longer dealing with a ghost story, but rather with an urban legend.

Popular adolescent urban legends include the horror tales of lovers' lanes, escaped lunatics and cars that won't start in terrifying circumstances.

I was assured, while still at junior school in Bloemfontein, that the following event occurred on Naval Hill, that landlocked city's rather inaptly named central landmark. There is an area on the mountain known as Hangman's Valley, and this is how it got its name:

The Boyfriend's Death

One night a young courting couple drove up Naval Hill to do in the car what their parents wouldn't allow them to do at home. The boyfriend decided to turn on the radio for a little romantic mood music.

Just then, a bulletin came over the air with the warning: a lunatic had escaped from Groendakkies (a local mental home), and had been seen in the Naval Hill vicinity. People were asked to keep away from the area. Alarmed, the couple decided to go back home immediately, but when they turned the key in the ignition the car wouldn't start. The boy decided to go for help. The girl begged him to take her with him.

Reluctant to take the chance, he assured her she would be all right if she lay on the back seat with a blanket over her. She was not to look up until he knocked three times on the window.

By and by, she heard the signal. Tap, tap, tap. She was about to get up, when the tapping continued. Tap, tap, tap, tap, tap. Terrified, she lay where she was.

Intermittently, the tapping would start again, in no particular pattern. Her boyfriend did not return. Finally, exhausted by terror, she fell asleep.

Next morning, she woke up to the sound of a great commotion. She sat up and saw that the car was surrounded by police cars. Seeing her, a policeman rushed over and told her to get out of the car and come with him, but under no circumstances to look back.

Of course, she did look back. And there was her boyfriend, hanging from a tree above the car, his shoes brushing against the car window. Tap, tap, tap.

I always knew this was a Bloemfontein, and specifically a Naval Hill story. Until I moved to Johannesburg, and discovered it was a Roodepoort story. And a Pretoria story. And a Boksburg story.

In fact, it is also an American story, told in virtually every town and city in the United States. It is also a German story, a Scandinavian story, an Australian and a British one.

A separate legend, sometimes tacked onto the Naval Hill story, is that the ghost of that murdered boy still haunts

Hangman's Valley, just in case kids need an extra reason for staying away from there.

An over-the-top Roodepoort version, which also refers to Groendakkies (*their* local mental hospital), has the girl waking to a hideous roaring. The car is surrounded by police, who coax her out. She looks back and sees the lunatic standing on the roof of the car, beating his chest, roaring, and swinging in his hand her boyfriend's severed head.

Another version of the story, reported by Jan Brunvand in *The Vanishing Hitchhiker*, was told by a University of Kansas student in the United States. It refers to highway 59, 'by the Holiday Inn', and concludes with the words: 'This is why the road is called Hangman's Road.' The location is extremely specific, as is the Naval Hill story: both places really do exist, and perhaps that road *is* known as Hangman's Road to the locals.

Any Bloemfontein resident will confirm the existence of Hangman's Valley, but as for the story that explains how the place got its name —? Pure urban legend, repeated a hundred thousand times in a hundred thousand places as a 'local story'.

(Incidentally, the 'real' origin of Hangman's Valley is allegedly the practice, ended many years before, of hanging convicted murderers in public on the mountain.)

Its message is simple: do not go to lonely spots to do things you shouldn't even be thinking of. The most hideous evil could befall you.

It is a cautionary tale that punishes the sexual transgressors in the ultimate way: with death and unforgettable horror. One would think that simple warnings about morality and teenage pregnancy would do the trick, but clearly irresponsible kids need to be shocked out of their skins before they will listen to wise adults.

The Hook

There are other Naval Hill stories. Today there is a tarred road up the hill, which skirts the top of the mountain and passes through Hangman's Valley before going down again. On one edge, the road looks out over the lights of Bloemfontein, and this particular stretch has always been a favourite of young lovers in parked cars. It still is today, despite the following true story.

The story begins, as before, with a couple who go up Naval Hill to look at the lights. The car radio is again playing romantic music. The night is warm with promise.

Suddenly a news flash interrupts the music. A lunatic has escaped from Groendakkies, and was last seen in the Naval Hill area. He can be recognised by the gruesome hook which he has in place of a hand.

The girl is nervous, but the boy is feeling amorous. He doesn't want to leave. She protests but he tries harder. She demands he remove his hands. He keeps them where they are. She reaches out and switches off the radio.

Next thing there's the sound of a scratch on the door. Terrified, the girl insists that they leave. The boy is furious and he pulls away with a squeal of tyres. At home, he goes round to the passenger door to open it for her and promptly passes out.

There, hanging from the door handle, is the bloody stump of the lunatic's hook.

On 8 November 1960, America's best known advice column, Dear Abby, printed this letter:

> DEAR ABBY: If you are interested in teenagers, you will print this story. I don't know whether it is true or not, but it doesn't matter because it served its purpose for me: A fellow and his date pulled into their favorite 'lover's

lane' to listen to the radio and do a little necking. The music was interrupted by an announcer who said there was an escaped convict in the area who had served time for rape and robbery. He was described as having a hook instead of a right hand. The couple became frightened and drove away. When the boy took his girl home, he went around to open the car door for her. There he saw – a hook on the door handle! I don't think I will ever park to make out as long as I live. I hope this does the same for other kids. JEANETTE.

Urban legends could have been designed with people like Jeanette in mind. She understood the message immediately, even if her reaction to the story was melodramatic. Urban legends do that to people.

These two particular varieties are usually told along with assorted ghost and horror stories, although ghosts as such are not involved. The mysterious, usually invisible murderer serves a supernatural function quite effectively.

American folklorist Alan Dundes ascribes serious Freudian overtones to the legend: the hook, he says, is a phallic symbol that penetrates the girl's door handle, but which is torn off when the car moves off abruptly. The girl's virtue is saved by insisting on being taken home, as a result of the radio message, which represents the voice of her conscience.

I suspect Jeanette would have approved of this interpretation.

There are many ghost stories which do not include ghosts or even ghostly surrogates.

This next story I recall first hearing on Ten o'Clock Tales, a Springbok Radio series which ran on Wednesday nights, and began with the tolling of ten mournful churchbells. Just the sound of those bells, before the listener had managed to leap for the off-switch, was enough to cause sleepless nights for adolescents.

The tales were purportedly dramatisations of experiences sent in by listeners. Most were common or garden ghost stories, and several were urban legends, like this one, broadcast in the early seventies:

The Haunted Nail

During the Second World War, a South African soldier on a French battlefield somewhere was persuaded to stand guard in a mortuary, apparently as a prank by his fellow-soldiers. In the mortuary lay the bodies of many deceased soldiers, arranged on benches, awaiting a decent burial.

Naturally, the soldier was nervous, but he was a soldier, and he would do his duty. That night, sitting on one of the benches in the swirling darkness, things began playing on his mind. He became increasingly nervous, suspecting every shadow, seeing movement in every flicker of light and darkness.

Suddenly, it all got too much for him and he leaped up, intending to run out. As he leaped to his feet, however, someone grabbed his jacket from behind and pulled him back. Completely terror-struck, the poor man had a heart attack and died.

The next morning his comrades saw him lying dead on the bench. On closer examination they found that his jacket had got caught on a nail sticking up out of the bench.

I heard the story again in 1987, although it seemed to have its origin in the 1950s. A friend told me that it had happened to a friend of his father's, while they were students at the University of the Witwatersrand medical school:

During orientation, or initiation, as it was then called, my father's friend had to spend the night in a haunted house somewhere in Johannesburg. Part of the dare was to go into the house and knock a nail into a table in one of the rooms, to prove he'd been there.

They dropped him off at midnight outside a spooky, big old house that was so dark inside, even the shadows threw shadows. He made his way with a small torch through the long, dark passages to the room with the table.

All the time, he could hear strange creaking sounds in the house. He was not to know it was the seniors trying to scare him and he started to get jumpy. Finally he found the room, but by this time he was so nervous he was ready to jump at any unexpected object, even a chair, which appeared in the light of his torch.

As he was knocking the nail into the table, he suddenly saw shadows moving in the room. They were caused by the hammering motion of his arm, but all logic had deserted him. His imagination was working overtime.

Deciding he wasn't going to spend another second in the house, he turned to run. Just then, someone grabbed him by his coat and jerked him back! He promptly died of a heart attack.

The next morning the seniors found him lying there, his coat stuck in the nail he had driven into the table.

This legend fits in well with a category of horror stories told about student pranks going wrong, particularly strong among medical students. While the Haunted Nail does not seem to be well known, another story is told by university students around the world. This version happened at Pretoria University:

The Body in the Bed

There was once a woman student studying medicine at Pretoria University who had the reputation of being very tough. She wasn't scared of anything, and would slice up a cadaver like she was slicing chicken.

One day some students in her class decided to find out how tough she really was. They stole the arm of a corpse out of a lab, sneaked it into her bedroom as she slept that night, and quietly placed it on the pillow beside her. Then they slipped out, and waited for her reaction.

The next morning they knocked on her door. There was no reply. They knocked again, and heard a groaning from inside. They rushed in, and there they saw her, sitting on top of the cupboard, with a wild look in her eyes, dribbling at the mouth, and groaning. In her hand she held the arm — half chewed.

The clear non-psychological purpose of such stories is to scare the hell out of fellow students, or at least to give them shivers up the spine during those late-night storytelling sessions adolescents and students delight in. There is also the underlying cautionary tale theme that playing pranks of this nature can have tragic consequences. And, of course, the element of confirming 'youth of today' irresponsibility.

However, such warnings, meanings and variations seem trivial in the light of the 'genuine' ghost stories which have made such a powerful impact on the public mind that they have become part of modern folklore.

The Uniondale Ghost

The best-known South African ghost story is undoubtedly the Lady in White, or the Uniondale Ghost. The tale is repeated in major South African magazines every few years, usually just before Easter.

This ghost even has a name: Maria Charlotte Roux, killed in a road accident near Uniondale in the Eastern Cape on 12 April 1968 at 4.30am one Easter morning.

According to the police report of the accident, the car was

driven by her fiancé, one GM Pretorius, 21 years old. He was driving at about 100km/h when he moved his right hand from the steering wheel and lost control of the car. Maria, who was asleep in the passenger seat, was flung from the car and killed.

The story is now taken up by David Barritt, a journalist who has written extensively about the case. Writing in the *Sunday Times* Magazine on 29 March 1987, he comments that it was a tragedy that would have been forgotten, except that people began seeing Maria's ghost:

> *Mr and Mrs Leonard Fraser from Cradock ... on Easter Friday 1973, were the first to see her.*
>
> *'We were on our way to Oudtshoorn,' said Mr Fraser. 'At around midnight I stopped the car on the Willowmore-Uniondale road and got out to stretch my legs. The road was deserted when I got out but suddenly a figure dressed in a long white dress appeared beside me. I got such a fright that I dived straight back into the car and drove off. As I tore off down the road I could still see the figure standing there.'*
>
> *... The most convincing account is that of Mr Anthony le Grange, then aged 41, who saw the ghost on 1 May 1976.*
>
> *At about 7.15 that night, Mr le Grange was driving along the Uniondale-Willowmore road when he saw a dark-haired girl, dressed in duffle coat and slacks, standing at the roadside. 'She wasn't hitch-hiking but because it was cold and raining I stopped the car,' he said. 'She opened the door and got in.*
>
> *'I noticed that her face was very pale.*
>
> *'I asked her where she wanted to go and she said "Porter Straat twee, de Lange." These are the only words she spoke to me.'*
>
> *Mr le Grange started his car and drove on. 'I didn't know where Porter Street was so I turned to ask her and*

she was gone.' He was nonplussed. 'I just didn't know what to do so I drove to Uniondale police station and reported what had happened.

'Of course the policeman didn't take my story seriously. He told me to forget it and continue my journey. I was mystified and confused but what could I do except do as he said. I got back in my car and carried on toward Oudtshoorn.

'Just outside Uniondale I heard the most chilling sound I have ever heard in my life. It was an hysterical scream of fear and shock and it came from inside my car. To me everything stopped, my flesh went cold and prickly and I felt as if I had no blood in my veins. I was completely terrified.

'At that time I had never heard of the girl ghost but now when I think about that scream I think I was hearing the sound the girl made at the time of the crash.

'I turned the car round and went straight back to the police station. I told the policeman what had happened and said, "Look, the woman is still in my car." I made him examine the car with me. We found nothing but there was no way I was going to drive off alone so I insisted the policeman follow me in his van.

'I drove off at a steady 70 km/h, after having first made sure all the doors were securely locked. The policeman followed closely behind me.

'Just outside Uniondale the right rear door of my car slowly opened and closed, exactly as if someone got out and then shut the door behind them. I stopped the car and the policeman came up to me and asked if I had seen it. All he could say over and over again was "How about that?" '

The policeman who witnessed what happened that night is Cornelius Potgieter, now a sergeant based in Vryheid, Natal. He confirmed Mr le Grange's story in every detail.

Barritt reports that Andries Vermeulen, who was then Uniondale's magistrate, launched an investigation. He collected sightings, and was given positive identification after showing a picture of Maria to the witnesses.

Barritt also spoke to a Uniondale resident, Charles van Rensburg, who claimed to have helped a University of Pretoria scientist investigate the sightings. Van Rensburg said the scientist eventually contacted the ghost, and told her she was dead and that her spirit was now free. 'Since then no one has seen the ghost,' said Van Rensburg.

Penny Miller's comprehensive collection of traditional folk stories, *Myths and Legends of Southern Africa*, published in 1979, includes the tale as 'The Spectral Hitchhiker'. She briefly tells the Le Grange version, and goes into further detail on another incident which had also been recorded by Barritt:

> *Mr Dawie van Jaarsveld from Johannesburg was going to visit his girlfriend at Oudtshoorn. He decided to take the road through De Rust, but it was growing dark and beginning to rain dismally. He had actually lost his way when he arrived at the first turn-off to Barendas. He was surprised when the headlights of his motorbike shone on the figure of a girl wearing dark slacks and a blouse. She was soaking wet as she stood watching him. Touched by her plight, he offered her a lift into town, and helped her don his spare crash-helmet; he even gave her an earphone so that she could listen to music as they rode. They set off briskly for Uniondale and travelled the next 17 kilometres to the second turn-off to Barendas. Just at that point he felt the back wheel skid slightly and thinking he might have a puncture he stopped to investigate. The girl had gone. With a growing sense of horror, he saw that the spare crash helmet was still firmly fastened to his motorbike and the earphone he had given her he found firmly plugged in his own ear! By*

*the time he reached the Petros cafe in Uniondale he was
in sore need of the cup of strong coffee that was given to
him.*

Barritt's version of the story places it on 31 March 1978. It
has Van Jaarsveld feeling 'something about her that made
my flesh go cold' before she climbed on the bike. As he was
driving along, he started feeling unnaturally cold, and
speeded up to 120km/h. When the wheel skidded slightly,
he looked in his rearview mirror to make sure the girl was all
right. She was gone. He thought she had fallen off and went
back to look for her, until he realised his spare helmet was
bouncing against his back. It was still clipped to the luggage
rack. Barritt does not mention the earphone.

Yet another version, reported by Cynthia Hind in *Fate*
magazine in July 1979, has Van Jaarsveld suspecting a flat
tyre, looking round, and seeing, or not seeing, the inevitable.

Hind went to the Petros cafe, where the proprietress
confirmed the man coming in 'like he'd seen a ghost' and
that he had claimed to have met the phantom hitch-hiker.

Hind also went to the ultimate destination mentioned in
versions she had heard: the Louterwater farm, where Van
Jaarsveld had been going to meet his girlfriend. Residents at
the farm confirmed that he had arrived in a nervous state
and that he had repeated his experience to them.

Cynthia Hind went to look up Constable Potgieter to
check up on Le Grange's story. Potgieter confirmed the
story, except that he said he had accompanied Le Grange
after the desperate man's first — not second — visit to the
police station. When the car door had opened, the constable
said, he had heard a maniacal laugh.

Meanwhile, a Lieutenant Giel Pretorius of the SA Air
Force contacted the press, claiming he had been the driver
of the car in the story's origin. He said his fiancée had been
flung from the car when a powerful wind threw it from the
road and flung it over an embankment. He produced a

photograph of his fiancée, which Mr le Grange said was a close resemblance, although he was not certain.

Hind also did the obvious: she went looking for 2 Porter Street. The only one on record in the Cape was in Worcester, and that was the addresss of a boys' hostel. She was unable to contact Lt Pretorius, or Maria Roux's mother, who had apparently moved elsewhere.

As mentioned before, this story is South Africa's best-known 'true' ghost story, and, despite all the seemingly factual evidence, it is also one of South Africa's best-known urban legends.

The case has fascinated folklorists, as it happens to be the best documented version in the world of one of the most enduring and widespread international urban legends.

Jan Brunvand even named his first book after this brand of urban legend: *The Vanishing Hitchhiker*. The book does not even mention the Uniondale ghost, there are so many others to choose from. The traditional version of the legend goes like this:

A man is driving on a lonely road one dark and stormy night. Peering ahead through his windscreen wipers, he suddenly sees a hitch-hiker at the side of the road. It is a young woman, wet and bedraggled from the rain.

He picks her up, and she gives him her address in the next town. After a while, he turns to speak to her — and she's gone. All that remains is a puddle of water where she had been sitting. Terrified, he speeds into the next town, and goes to the address she had given. A man opens the door, takes one look at the traveller's face, and says sadly, 'You gave my daughter a ride, didn't you?'

Astonished, the traveller asks how he knew. The father says this is not the first time. His daughter had died in a motor accident ten years ago on the same spot where she'd been hitch-hiking on this night, and she had been trying to get back ever since. He thanks the traveller for having tried to bring her home.

The Uniondale ghost fits the legend perfectly, except that the travellers never get to meet the parents. Ironically, however, the 'true' story has passed into the general pool of South African urban legends in exactly the version involving the parents.

It is told as having happened to travellers in various parts of the country, and usually includes the parents meeting the traveller at the door. In one version, which I recall hearing on radio but have been unable to track down, the traveller knocks on the door, tells the parents he had given their daughter a lift and she had disappeared. That's impossible, they say. She had died exactly a year ago, in a motor accident. Suddenly he sees, over their shoulders, a portrait on the wall of a young woman: the hitch-hiker he had given a ride.

A different approach to the legend has a young man driving across the country, usually from Cape Town to Johannesburg or from Johannesburg to Durban:

The traveller is exhausted, and finds he can hardly stay awake, but he has to get to his destination by the next morning, and cannot stop to rest. He sees a hitch-hiker on the side of the road, and thinks that perhaps having company will help keep him awake.

He gives a ride to the hiker, a young man. The man is rather tense, and every five minutes he asks the driver the time. The driver gets quite irritated, but eventually finds himself waiting in anticipation for the next query.

By the time he sees the lights of Joahnnesburg (or Durban) he is wide awake. He turns to the hiker to make some comment ... and the man is gone.

The next day, at a meeting, he recounts this strange experience. Another man at the meeting, suddenly wide-eyed, says, 'That was my son!'.

It turns out that his son had died on that same road some years before after falling asleep behind the wheel. Every now and then, his father would come across someone who had picked up a hitch-hiker, who in turn had kept the driver awake throughout a long trip by constantly asking for the time, or striking up conversations relating to getting home safely.

Penny Miller, in *Myths and Legends of South Africa*, tells of another female ghost hiker, supposedly haunting the verges of Du Toits Kloof in the Western Cape. But this one is rather more difficult to authenticate because 'whoever takes her in their car is always involved in a fatal accident'.

Jan Brunvand classifies these legends under 'Roadside Ghosts'. The Vanishing Hitchhiker, he says, is a prime example of the adaptability of urban legends. It is also the classic automobile legend. 'This returning-ghost tale was known by the turn of the century both in the United States and abroad,' he says. 'It acquired the newer automobile motif by the period of the Great Depression, and thereafter spawned a number of subtypes ... some of which themselves stemmed from earlier folk tales.'

All the accounts traced by Brunvand were told as 'true' stories, which supposedly happened to friends of the narrators. No less than fifteen distinct plots are recorded, with numerous variants of each plot. One of them, involving the portrait-identification element, has been traced back to St Petersburg, Russia, in 1890. It was actually reported in a Russian newspaper called *The Citizen*, published on 16 December 1890. It does not involve cars, but instead a priest who is asked by a woman in the street to give sacraments to a sick man at a certain address. The priest goes to the house, but the healthy-looking man who lets him in doesn't know what he's talking about. The priest then sees a portrait on the wall. He points to it. That was the person who had made the

110

request, he says. It is a portrait of the man's long-dead mother. In terror, the young man takes communion from the priest. That night, he dies.

'The quest for the ultimate origin of the Vanishing Hitchhiker and its variations pretty well comes to a halt at this point,' says Brunvand, 'at least until further nineteenth century and foreign prototypes are discovered. But updated and localized treatments of the legend continue to flourish in modern folklore, suggesting that the old ghost tale must have some important appeal to contemporary folk.'

Brunvand draws attention to a prototype, which he insists is not related to the modern hitch-hiker, in the New Testament, *Acts* 8:26-39. An Ethiopian in a chariot gives a ride to Apostle Philip, who baptises him, then disappears.

If you're still not convinced that the Uniondale ghost is an urban legend, perhaps you need a close encounter with a book called *The Evidence for Phantom Hitch-hikers*, by Michael Goss. It is published by the Aquarian Press in conjunction with the Association for the Scientific Study of Anomalous Phenomena, and investigates the numerous hitch-hiker stories told around the world, from New Zealand to New York.

Goss comments that 'the 100-plus (stories) upon which this present book draws is far from an exhaustive sample.

'Taken as a group, the individual variations within these hitch-hiker narratives do not disguise the obvious fact that we are dealing basically with the same story.'

The real contrasts in the stories lie in the way they conclude. Most end up explaining exactly who the ghost was, while others defy us to find a better explanation.

Goss has one warning which should be a red flag to Uniondale believers: '... folklore warns us that in hitch-hiker stories police involvement is flourished as another pseudo-corroborative narrative element, one that enhances the credibility of an inherently incredible tale; by that the police took the thing seriously we are led to believe that the preceding part of the narrative was "serious" (authentic) as well.'

Goss discovers that 'there have been cases featuring named witnesses, some of them subsequently interviewed by investigators who found no blatant evidence of fabrication.'

The Uniondale ghost is given extensive coverage by Goss. He discusses an earlier version by David Barritt, from the 18 July 1980 edition of *Scope*, as well as Cynthia Hinds' investigation for *Fate* magazine.

He comments: 'Looking with some difficulty past the assorted discrepancies in these accounts — applauding also that someone went to the trouble of trying to check the story by interviewing available witnesses ... it depends as usual on the credibility of unsupported eyewitnesses, but there are two of them, two reporters and two separate incidents pointing in the direction of a ghost that obeys the folklore tenets concerning the tragic origins and regularized (anniversary) appearances.'

Goss's final conclusion about the legend is that 'there is sound evidence pointing to the Phantom Hitchhiker being a classic fabrication — a supernatural tale told as a matter of truth because that is part of the narrative convention.

'Outside that convention, the story is obviously not true: (it is an) urban legend.'

And if you are still not convinced, perhaps the time has come to contact the person who has spent more time than any other researching the Uniondale ghost, David Barritt.

When I went to see him he kindly dug out his records on one of the most popular stories he had ever written. He answered several of the questions foremost in my mind — not to mention the minds of many folklorists who have examined the reports, but have never bothered to question the reporter.

First of all, why did none of the stories ever quote the

parents, except in one brief mention that has the mother moving to another town? Why was the fiancé only brought in second-hand, and never actually quoted? Why was there no awareness of the international nature of this story?

Barritt confirmed that he did contact the parents, but the moment they heard what he was calling about, they refused to speak to him. 'I do definitely remember contacting her former fiancé, Pretorius,' Barritt said. 'He didn't want to discuss the matter either, saying she was dead and should be left in peace.'

Barritt has seen his story published many times. The original target of his article was the American sensationalist tabloid *National Enquirer*, which immediately puts a question mark to how seriously the story can be taken. Barritt himself did not deny this, but pointed out that the *Enquirer* went through a stage 'where they wanted every claim checked up as thoroughly as possible — and they paid for it. I had the luxury of going down to Uniondale in 1978 and spending some time in the Eastern Cape following up the various leads.'

Barritt's most reliable witness was Le Grange, not only because his story was backed up by both Potgieter and a second policeman on duty that night, but also because of what happened to Le Grange next.

'This is the part I really like about the story,' he said. 'Le Grange's wife told me that before that night he was a hard-drinking rabble-rouser. Overnight, there was a complete metamorphosis. He gave up drinking, and became a churchgoer, which he never had been.'

Barritt further revealed, however, that the story told by the other witness, Van Jaarsveld, had not stood the test of time quite as well.

'I think he was not the most reliable of witnesses. He contacted me some time later to say he'd seen other ghosts. I wouldn't put a high credibility rating on his story.'

Having spoken to the people involved and the people

who witnessed the reactions of those people, did Barritt believe this was the one authentic version of the vanishing hitch-hiker?

'Firstly, I don't believe in ghosts,' he said adamantly. 'But that story made more of an impression on me than any other I've written — largely because of the testimony of Le Grange and the policemen I spoke to, as well as the Frasers, who were the first to report seeing the girl.

'The stories weren't second-hand. They were the first-hand testimony of three highly credible people who didn't have any reason to make up a story. There were no friends of friends involved. People like Le Grange have never heard of urban legends. He was a simple fellow. But something happened that night that changed his life profoundly.'

Michael Goss cuts to the heart of the matter when he says that, even if a witness does report the experience to the police, and the police do respond, and it goes on record, 'we can still dismiss the thing: police involvement or not, there is still absolutely no guarantee that the witness was speaking the truth. And even if he was, the truth as he perceived it may not correspond with the truth of what actually happened.'

No matter which way you turn, as far as the sceptical enquirer is concerned, you still lose.

On the other hand, perhaps the phantom hitch-hiker is very real, and she's still out there, standing by the Barendas turn-off, waiting forlornly in the rain for the next unwitting traveller — perhaps you? — to give her a ride.

10   FOOD FOR FEARS

Little awakens our subconscious fears as effectively as the thought of a secret contamination in our bodies. Horror stories of dangerous objects or poisons hidden in food, of medicines gone wrong, the shocking consequences of fad diets, make for riveting tales. The press thrives on them, knowing how compelling they are to readers.

It should come as no surprise, therefore, to find a rich vein of food fear running through urban legends.

South Africans, as always, have a special way with these legends, often bringing in the subtleties of a worldview that reflects their political isolation. Most legends do retain their international flavour, but occasionally the topical touch gives it the edge that transforms an ordinary urban legend into a great one.

I was told the following story in all earnestness.

The Kentucky Fried Rat

This happened about two years ago at the height of the sanctions campaign, when many companies were disinvesting in South Africa. People kept looking for clues that a company was about to pull out.

Kentucky Fried Chicken suddenly launched a new advertising campaign with new characters replacing Colonel Saunders — I think they were a wolf and a crow. So people said they were planning a name change, and were familiarising the public with their new image, as the parent company was going to disinvest.

Well, Kentucky refuted the name change claim, but they

did finally announce their disinvestment. The workers at the Hillbrow branch were really furious, because they thought they were now going to lose their jobs.

So they put rats in the batter. People didn't notice the difference, because it tasted just as good. But someone got sick while they were eating it, and took a closer look, and that's how it came out.

This tale is so bizarre, it didn't gain too much currency. Corporate sabotage is one thing, but a rat would be a little difficult to disguise as a fried chicken drumstick. No one could possibly believe this story. Or could they?

A full decade before the legend became politicised, American talkshow host Johnny Carson told his audience that a woman was suing a fast food chain for serving her a 'batter-fried-rat'. That was in May 1979. An even earlier version dates to 1971. Collected by Maryland folklorist George G Carey, it went like this:

Two couples stopped one night at a notable carry-out for a fried chicken snack. The husband returned to the car with the chicken. While sitting there in the car eating their chicken, the wife said: 'My chicken tastes funny.' She continued to eat and continued to complain.

After a while her husband said, 'Let me see it.' The driver of the car decided to put the light on and it was discovered that the woman was eating a rodent, nicely flavoured and fried crisp. The woman went into shock and was rushed to the hospital. It was reported that the husband was approached by lawyers representing the carry-out and offered the sum of $35 000 (to keep quiet about it). The woman remained on the critical list for several days. Spokesmen from the hospital would not divulge the facts about the case and nurses were instructed to keep their mouths shut. And it is also reported that a second offer was made for $75 000, and this too was refused. The woman died and presumably the case will come to court.

Jan Brunvand says of this particular legend, 'the specific setting and dialogue in the tale, the references to the suppression of information, and the exact dollar figures offered to the victims are hallmarks of the fully-fledged urban legend.'

Yet again, a folklorist has made an elaborate study of 'Kentucky Fried Rat' legends, analysing 115 versions. Professor Gary Alan Fine, of the University of Minnesota, discusses among these variations an example in which disgruntled fast-food workers fry mice or even cats in batter. The South African version obviously has a long pedigree.

After Kentucky Fried Chicken (incidentally, the secret herbs and spices recipe is designed to mask the rat flavour), the most constant corporate butt of food legends is Coca Cola.

Rat Cola

The fact that strange objects do turn up in soft drinks from time to time gives credibility to legends of rats or even half-rats — it's difficult to decide which is worse — turning up in the bottom of Coke bottles.

The legends have an added advantage: rats really *have* turned up in Coke bottles, or at least one rat, as attested to in a court case reported in the *Washington Post* on 3 February 1971.

A 76-year-old man, George Petalas, was awarded $20 000 for the insult, which he said had left him 'permanently sickened'. The judge decided that the bottle must have been tampered with, but ruled that Petalas had to be compensated for 'mental anguish'.

Fine has traced genuine Rat Cola court cases back to

1914, when the judge went as far as to quote Robert Burns' poem 'To A Mouse' in the court. In all, forty-four cases had been appealed up to 1976.

Interestingly, while the victims in urban legends are usually women, who usually expire, the court cases are usually brought by men, who usually survive.

Dental Cola

The many alleged medicinal properties of Coca Cola would make for a respectable body of modern folklore. It is said to induce abortion (when forced into the womb) and cure indigestion (when left open to go flat). It is supposedly capable of dissolving a chunk of meat within hours. One story going around in the 1970s had it that, if you left a 2c piece in a glass of Coke overnight, it too would dissolve. My father once disproved this power when he left an old coin in a saucer of Coke overnight. That the coin survived wasn't much comfort: it had been left in the Coke to dissolve hard-caked rust that had collected on the coin.

And so we come to the legend of the old lady and the Dental Cola, a favourite tale in homes where 'good help is so hard to get'.

There was an old lady who used to keep her dentures in a certain liquid that looked like Coke. One day her maid knocked the glass over by mistake. Hoping her employer wouldn't notice, she replaced the liquid with Coke. That night, when the old lady went to bed, she automatically dropped her dentures into the glass.

When she woke up next morning, she found beside her bed a glass of Coke containing a pile of loose teeth.

Commie Cola

An urban legend more difficult to trace, let alone find evidence for, is that of the communist onslaught in our cola. While I could find no one who remembers the exact details, this is what the tale boiled down to:

In the 1970s white schoolchildren were told by some teachers not to drink Coca Cola. Not only was it bad for the health, but it financed the enemies of South Africa. How so? Well, Coca Cola was a communist company, as proven by the red in its logo and on its merchandise. Getting school children to drink Coke not only made money for the communists, but also indoctrinated South African children to feeling sympathetic towards communism.

The indoctrination must have worked. On 2 February 1990, President FW de Klerk unbanned the SA Communist Party. Since they have not subsequently brought down Civilisation As We Know It, the SACP has receded just a little in the white consciousness as a source of paranoia.

In the 1960s and 1970s, however, things were a little different. South Africa was arguably at its most repressive, with a government which tried to legislate the very conversations that individuals were allowed to hold with one another.

A climate of hatred, suspicion, fear and paranoia was engendered as an effective mechanism for creating a form of unity among white South Africans, enabling the Government to proceed with the disastrous social engineering programme called Apartheid. One of the rallying points was the fight against the agents of communism or, as then army chief General Magnus Malan labelled it, the Total Onslaught. Every conceivable propaganda tool and scheme was used to drum the dangers of communism into South African heads.

At the notorious Veld Schools — South Africa's answer to summer camp — 'youth preparedness' was the banner under which children were told that pop music and blue jeans were weapons of the communist onslaught.

Since these represent youth culture, it is not hard to understand conservative-minded, pro-Government and hardline establishment-oriented teachers equating such objects with communism.

But Coca Cola? And just because it uses the colour red? That would immediately damn anyone from Colgate to Mobil to Liverpool FC. Perhaps there is a more logical link in the chain of paranoia, but it is more tenuous, and highly speculative.

In the 1930s and 1940s, before the National Party came to power, most of the woes of South Africa's white working class were blamed on foreign capital, allegedly bent on exploiting the struggling Afrikaner. When the NP won the 1948 general election, they threatened to nationalise all industry in an effort to redress what they saw as the economic imbalances in the country.

In the end they settled for a subtle brand of socialism in a capitalist-dominated system, but the suspicion of international big business never disappeared completely from the thinking of more conservative elements of the establishment.

And what better symbol of international big business than Coca Cola? It is the very embodiment of American corporate imperialism. As a foreign infiltrator, it becomes, by extension, part of the Total Onslaught and thus a camp-follower of communism. And thus we have Commie Cola, the Red Thing.

The other side of the paranoia coin is a very unsubtle xenophobia, which reveals itself in urban legends about ethnic minorities, immigrants and foreigners in general. While South Africa is fertile breeding ground for such legends, there is nothing original in local versions. They are usually time-honoured stories that have their counterparts in possibly every major city in the world.

For its local colour, this is my favourite version of...

The Chinese Chicken Bone

Now this really did happen, but you can't write about it, because there was a court case and the chap had to pay a fine. I think he can sue you if you write about it now.

What happened was a family went to eat in one of those Chinese restaurants at the bottom of Commissioner Street — you know, near John Vorster Square. The wife ordered chicken, and she was still busy eating when a bone got stuck in her throat. She was rushed to the hospital, and the doctor managed to get the bone out. He examined it, and then asked her what she had been eating.

She said, 'Chicken.' He said, 'Let me ask you again what were you eating?' She again said, 'Chicken.'

He replied: 'I'm afraid not, lady. This is a cat bone.' She sued the restaurant and I think she was awarded R20 000.

This is one of the most popular food legends in South Africa. The same day I heard the above version, someone told me substantially the same story set in Greece, and shortly thereafter I heard a (supposedly) first-hand account from someone who knew someone to whom it had happened in New York. In fact, one of my more cynical correspondents put it this way:

A lady had dinner one evening at a new Chinese restaurant in Johannesburg. Strangely enough, a similar event occurred in Durban, London, New York, Amsterdam and ten thousand other venues, so I am unable to vouch for the authenticity of this story.

She was enjoying a meat dish when suddenly she choked.

121

A bone had lodged in her throat and she couldn't breathe. They rushed her to hospital where she was immediately attended to, anaesthetised and operated upon.

The doctor casually asked the husband what she had been eating for supper and the man said that his wife had had a light soup followed by a Chinese chicken dish.

'Strange, that,' mused the doctor. 'Wonder why there was a cat's bone in her throat?'

Well may he wonder. The legend is directly related to the popular joke that Chinese restaurants habitually serve cat and dog meat. This myth is related to the fact that in the Far East animals we regard as pets are fair game for the dinner table.

A recent photo feature on China published in *Time Magazine* included a scene in a butcher's shop, showing a customer inspecting a live puppy while a dog's carcass hangs in the background. The photo generated a storm of outraged letters. The revulsion that many people in the West feel for such practices finds its ideal expression in urban legends.

It is unlikely that a Chinese restaurant has ever been directly accused of serving cat meat in South Africa, but it is equally unlikely that the legend will die a quiet death. Besides an opportunity for condemning Oriental custom, it also gives vent to general distrust — at least among conservative or racist whites — of Chinese people or, for that matter, of anyone who would not be classified white under present South African law.

Chinese people, until not long ago, were classified as 'honorary whites'. Even so, or perhaps because of this, they were still barred from a variety of 'whites only' facilities, in particular municipal swimming pools. Schools in some country towns also refused to admit Chinese children as recently as May 1990.

While there may be several avenues for expressing such

racism, the urban legend is the most inoffensive and socially harmless — at first glance.

The Chinese Chicken Bone is a perennial American urban legend, and takes on new elements from time to time. The influx of Vietnamese refugees during the 1970s and 1980s has changed the focus a little, and has even, in some cases, given the legend a solidity it doesn't deserve.

In one American community, otherwise respectable citizens heard and believed rumours of domestic cats disappearing and their entrails being found in the dustbins of Vietnamese homes. Police were called upon to act on the reports, and of course found no evidence to back up any of the allegations. This case proved that urban legends can have a profoundly negative impact on anyone who is connected, however spuriously, with the basic elements of the myth. Even where authorities may dismiss an allegation, the suspicion — and the resultant discrimination — remains.

This does not mean that telling an urban legend is a racist act. Far from it. It may even be a mechanism for otherwise enlightened people to come to terms with their latent racist feelings. Being able to laugh at those feelings makes it easier to face them, and thus to get rid of them.

Urban legend as social healer? That is perhaps not such a difficult thought to swallow.

11 DEATH, DRUGS AND DIET PILLS

You do not need a menu to tell you that most of the legends in the previous chapter deal with the dangers of eating in exotic or fast-food restaurants. A hidden warning seems to be: 'Eat at home, with your family, in a traditional setting, and you will come to no harm.'

Unfortunately, even this advice cannot save you from yourself, as the following correspondent informed me.

The Poisoned Pet

A couple who had emigrated to South Africa from England had one ambition: they wanted to gather fresh mushrooms in the fields of their farm, and cook and eat them straight away. Friends told them that if they chose the dark-bottomed mushrooms and left the light-bottomed ones alone, they would be quite safe. Only the light ones were poisonous.

They followed this advice, but once they had cooked them, fed some to their dog, just to be sure. After two hours the dog was still running around cheerfully, so they assumed the mushrooms were 'safe' and went on to enjoy their meal.

Later in the afternoon an African man not fluent in English came and told them their dog was dead. Panic-stricken, the couple rushed the 20 kilometres to the nearest doctor, who gave them an injection and had them flown 200 kilometres to a hospital where their stomachs were pumped. After this panic, and the considerable expense involved, the couple returned home to find that their dog had not died of mushroom poisoning — it had been run over by a car.

The moral of the story? Never trust a dog? Or never trust a farmhand? Or never trust people who can't speak your language? Or simply beware of picking mushrooms even when you think they're safe.

The legend is interesting from the point of view that it apparently began in traditional folklore. A powerful man, possibly a king, had a food-taster who died after tasting a particular meal. The benign employer immediately had his chef put to death, only to discover the taster had died of other causes.

In recent years, this tale evolved into an anecdote of the after-dinner-speech variety:

At a dinner party, a guest feeds a morsel of smoked salmon to the family cat. The creature instantly begins coughing and gasping before keeling over and, to all appearances, proceeding to choke slowly to death. The host and guests are appalled, and there is much panic as they are all rushed to hospital to have their stomachs pumped. Meanwhile, the cat finally gags up its hairball, and cheerfully hops onto the table to finish off the rest of the half-eaten salmon.

From this 'joke' version, the story has returned to folklore, of the urban variety, completing an unusual cycle of oral evolution.

The anecdotal version of the story has a curious link with another category of contamination legends: strange objects and organisms found in people's stomachs. While medical history is littered with forceps and knives left behind in patients' insides after operations, urban legends prefer more unlikely objects, which make their way into our bodies by very obvious and vulnerable pathways.

125

The Deadly Hairball

In *The Mexican Pet*, Jan Brunvand records the story of a barber who dies in unusual circumstances and an investigation is required. An autopsy reveals large hairballs in his lungs. The conclusion? The hairballs had formed from hair he had breathed in during his years of cutting people's hair. Eventually the accumulation suffocated him.

Just in case I had any confusion about the intention of the story, a friend lent me a worn copy of a book called *Cautionary Verses*, by Hilaire Belloc, published in 1940. It includes 'Cautionary Tales for Children', 'New Cautionary Tales' and a 'Moral Alphabet'. The second tale in the book is headlined 'Henry King, Who chewed bits of String, and was early cut off in Dreadful Agonies'.

> *The Chief Defect of Henry King*
> *Was chewing little bits of string.*
> *At last he swallowed some which tied*
> *Itself in ugly knots inside.*
> *Physicians of the Utmost Fame*
> *Were called at once; but when they came*
> *They answered, as they took their Fees,*
> *'There is no Cure for this Disease.*
> *Henry will very soon be dead.'*
> *His parents stood about his Bed*
> *Lamenting his Untimely Death,*
> *When Henry, with his Latest Breath,*
> *Cried – ,'Oh, my Friends, be warned by me,*
> *That Breakfast, Dinner, Lunch and Tea*
> *Are all the Human Frame requires...'*
> *With that the Wretched Child expires.*

Nowadays we hear stories of octopus, snakes and worse residing in stomachs. They generally enter in eggs, hatch out and attach themselves to stomach walls or curl around protuberances, living off body fat and growing, and finally showing up as tumours or suchlike on X-ray plates. The stomachs are cut open, and the horrible truth is revealed.

While this is no way for any creature to be raised, it confirms the urban legend view of the human subconscious.

Such legends have a long pedigree, going back to European folklore, which inserts snakes, frogs and other creatures in human bodies. Brunvand calls these 'Bosom-Serpent' legends, and the most recent variety certainly lives up to its name:

The Worm in the Diet Pill

An enterprising company put out guaranteed weight-loss diet pills a few years ago. Sure enough, the pills worked very well. Then they began to work too well. The authorities were called in, and it was found that the pills contained the heads of tapeworms.

The solution was to starve the person for a few days, and have him or her sit with his or her mouth open in front of a bowl of milk. This the tapeworm would smell, and out it would come.

Well, it really did happen. Or at least, I'm sure it did. I clearly remember reading about a legal case related to tapeworms in diet pills. It was in the *Sunday Times*, sometime between 1980 and 1986.

This is how it went:

Apparently, an entrepreneur in the Eastern Transvaal launched a revolutionary new diet pill on the market. He sold it by mail order, particularly through the *Sunday Times*.

They were effective in some cases, but in others made people very ill. After examining one of these patients, a doctor discovered that she had a tapeworm in her stomach. Legal proceedings were launched against the entrepreneur, who denied that he was doing anything illegal. And that was how the story ended. For all we know, this man is still selling tapeworms in diet pills to this day.

My informants in the world of medical research confirm this story ... almost. Zoologist Juliet Dear told me that while studying parasitology at the University of the Witwatersrand, her lecturer had brought this case up during a lecture, not to analyse it, but simply to report that it had happened in the United States, and that it was extremely irresponsible of the diet pill manufacturer ...

However, in this case they were not tapeworm heads — they were tapeworm eggs, which was even more dangerous. You see, the lecturer informed her class, the newly-hatched worms do not necessarily go to the intestines. They make their way into the brain, and cause irreversible brain damage.

Dear did not dismiss the legend entirely. 'It's believable,' she said, 'because some women will go to any lengths to lose weight.'

Medical research is given as the validating authenticity for many urban legends. If you are fond of dining out, skip the next few paragraphs.

After-dinner Substance

There was a series of tests in restaurants on various substances, specifically testing for uric acid. They discovered that the highest content of uric acid was found on the surface of peppermints given away at the exit. They concluded that many diners, especially men, will take a handful from the dishes of peppermints — shortly after they have visited the toilet at the end of their meal.

As a result, the Spur steakhouse chain installed dispensers which give out only one mint at a time.

I was told the story by a well-known journalist, who pointed out that he didn't really believe it, but knew people who did. Another informant told me that researchers had tested for fourteen different bacteria that are required to reveal the presence of urine. All fourteen were present.

Why the mysterious 'they' would want to test specifically for urine, when there are so many more noxious contaminants in our food, is a mystery, or perhaps just a shortcoming of that variation.

I have been told, quite solemnly, that 'they' have tested peppermints in restaurants and found them covered with a wide variety of appalling substances, including urine, semen and sweat.

The information usually follows the comment, 'You should never take peppermints in restaurants. You know what they've found on them?'

This legend ties in directly with the fast-food and foreign food legends, reflecting secret paranoias about eating in strange places, or in places where complete strangers share your space.

It is equally a legend of the devious ways in which disgusting contaminants cheat their way into the body.

Take this next cautionary tale for our times, not to mention our continent. Documented around the world as pure folklore, simpler truths lurk at its heart. This is the South African version, as told by Gus Silber in the August 1987 edition of *Style* magazine. Sensitive readers are advised to move on to the next chapter.

The Spider Bite

This chick from Sandton spends a weekend at a very expensive private game lodge on top of a koppie in the Kruger Park. It's like heaven, only with animals. She could stay there forever. If it wasn't for the animals. Those that aren't invisible are boring, and you have to get up at five in the morning to see them anyway.

So on the last day, when everyone else is pretending to enjoy the potholes and the fleeting smudges of frightened game, she rises at eight and annexes the poolside for her own exclusive use. Oiled, topless, splayed like a starfish, she falls asleep in the heat of the throbbing sun.

She is woken by a sharp stinging sensation, the lip-biting feeling of a hair suddenly plucked from the back of her neck. She slaps herself in reflex and stares at a spider running down her arm. Big, red, hairy. She screams.

Later, the game ranger is tender and reassuring. She will not only survive, she will flourish. Many spiders bite. Had this one been poisonous, she would have died within minutes. 'Serves you right for not coming on the game drive, hey?' And he winks.

In Sandton, in civilisation, the little red pinprick on her neck gets bigger by the day, and the doctor prescribes antibiotics. Why not? Her hypochondria may as well be consoled.

The bump on her neck is hot and pulpy to the touch. It disturbs her social equilibrium, but it causes her no pain. One night, half-asleep in a steaming-hot bath, she hears a tiny pop, just a whisper of air behind her ear.

She feels something crawling softly down her shoulder: something more than sweat. The mirror almost shatters with her scream. Dozens upon dozens of red, hairy baby spiders, scurrying from their surrogate womb.

Once again, the legend reflects a fear of unseen or unknown contamination within our bodies. Variants include spiders in hairdos and ants in sinuses.

Brunvand includes it under 'Bosom Serpents', relating a popular variety in modern American folklore: 'A woman tourist falls asleep on a Mexican beach, and a spider bites into her arm and lays an egg there ... the resulting boil on her arm eventually must be lanced, whereupon hundreds of tiny spiders come running out.' Brunvand has even found variations in the writings of Nathaniel Hawthorne (1843) and Henry David Thoreau (1851).

Every version, like the Kruger Park story, seems specific about the location, and it usually relates to popular vacation destinations among people in the area where a specific variation is told.

Paul Smith, in *The Book of Nastier Legends*, tells this British version:

> *A girl I know from Glasgow went on holiday with friends to the coast of North Africa – she had a terrific time. The only problem they had during the visit was on the last day when they had an invasion of small insects – particularly spiders. These appeared to have been blown out to the coast from the desert and all you could do was to keep brushing them away.*
>
> *In spite of this they managed to get a few hours' sunbathing in, during which my friend was bitten on her face by the spiders a couple of times. Thinking no more about it, she simply applied an antiseptic cream to the bites and forgot about them.*
>
> *By the time she had returned to Glasgow, the bites were looking rather inflamed and beginning to look like boils. In spite of further treatment, they refused to subside so she eventually thought it best to arrange to visit the doctor the following day.*
>
> *Going to the bathroom the next morning she saw in the*

mirror that the bites looked even worse. She had just begun to carefully wash her face when she felt a sharp pricking sensation. Looking in the mirror again she was horrified and began to scream hysterically. The boils had burst and crawling all over her face and in her hair were hundreds of tiny baby spiders.

Smith pointed out that the story had circulated in the UK since the mid-seventies, always set abroad at some exotic holday resort. '...it airs our prejudices against "foreign" customs,' he says. 'After all, they don't have the same standards of hygiene as us, do they?'

It is also an ideal cautionary tale to lay on any person about to embark on a trip to foreign climes, or game parks. The Kruger Park variation says more about the pampered nature of white suburbia than it does about foreign customs, and is probably an indicator of the increasing isolation of some elements of white society. Cloistered in their homes, behind high security walls, burglar alarms and floodlit gardens, they are safe from the world out there.

The moment they step out of this cocoon, into its diametric opposite — the wilds of Africa — they are courting danger, death and, even worse, contamination.

Or so we say.

In fact, something similar really has happened, and apparently happens all the time.

Gwen Gill, a popular columnist on the *Sunday Times*, informed me that while she lived in Central Africa she was warned of a grub that lives on guava trees. Somehow it gets onto wet washing and, if clothes are not ironed properly, it will get into your skin, where it lays its eggs. Precisely that happened to her:

'I thought I had chicken pox. There were bumps all over my back. I was rushed to a doctor, who recognised the bumps. He squeezed out forty-eight worms from my back.'

She knew of a man who, during the Congo war, had these

132

eggs buried so deep in his neck, he thought it was a bad boil before he had it treated.

Clearly, what has happened here is that a bizarre occurrence reported in isolated areas has reached the ears of urban dwellers, who have found in it something that speaks to their secret fears. In the telling and retelling, various elements have been added — suspicion of foreigners, fear of the great outdoors — until it has evolved into a full-blown urban legend.

Even if it really did happen.

12

EVERYTHING YOU
ALWAYS HEARD
ABOUT SEX ...

One of the most popular and universal themes in books, plays and motion pictures is sex. Why should urban legends be any different? They even have a moral purpose, which cannot be said of most screen or literary sex.

The guilty parties in sexual legends usually tend to get their come-uppance, whether in the form of physical injury, mortal embarrassment or eternal exile. The stories are the type of moral tales one would expect coming from older, perhaps more conservative, narrators. However, they are told with relish by young men and women on campuses, at offices and in pubs everywhere.

The following story, however, is not an urban legend. It really happened to the brother of a gentleman, by the name of Mark T. (he knows who he is), I knew at university. At least, he said it did...

The Nude Surprise Party

When my brother turned twenty-one, it was a Friday, and my parents couldn't get out of a dinner arrangement they'd made for that night. They apologised, and said they'd make it up to him.

He wasn't hassled though, because he wanted to have some PT with his girlfriend. The moment my folks left, he climbed into his woman. They went for it like a steamtrain, and after about the fourth time they were lying back, getting their breath, when the phone rang downstairs.

She didn't want him to go, so he said I'll be the horse, you be my rider, and we'll go answer the phone together. He gets up and she jumps on his back, and he piggybacks her downstairs, in the dark, and they haven't got a stitch of clothing on.

They get to the phone, and as he picks it up, all the lights go on. There are my folks, their best friends, old schoolbuddies of my brother, everyone — 'Surprise!' I wasn't there at the time, but I never heard the end of it.

To be perfectly honest, I haven't heard the end of it either. I heard this version in 1980, and have heard dozens since, although never attributed to a close living relative. It is sometimes told as a joke, but mostly as a supposedly true story.

The earliest South African version I have come across dates back to the 1950s, and is set in Cape Town. My informant only vaguely recalled it from his youth, but these details were clear in his memory: 'It was a surprise party for an engaged couple. The phone rings, it's dark, they come down the stairs. He's naked, she's on his shoulders, also naked. And the lights go on and it's a party. The actual couple were mentioned, but I don't remember the names. Also, it was just not allowed, premarital sex, even if you were engaged.'

Most versions include an engaged couple. They are on the verge of legal sex, but obviously cannot wait any longer, or never bothered to wait in the first place. But urban legend morality is merciless, and they must pay for their indiscretion. A 1970s version illustrates the unchanging laws of this morality:

An engaged couple. An empty house. A dream, or a nightmare? A girl was told by her parents that they would be going out one evening, leaving her alone at home. She telephoned her fiancé and invited him over. He arrived as

135

her parents were leaving. As some engaged couples do, they went to her room, undressed and made love.

The telephone rang. Who should answer it? 'Let's both go,' was the decision and so, both stark naked, the young man carried his girl into the kitchen to answer the phone.

As they walked into the kitchen, forty happy voices shouted, 'Surprise — kitchen tea!'

This is a little tame in the face of a 1980s version I received in the mail. By now, sex had left the bedroom and ventured into the bathroom:

Now this really, really happened to my cousin's best friend's sister's aunt ... Girl and guy are engaged. She lives with her parents who are going away for the weekend.

Guy comes over, after parents have left, to spend a dirty weekend filled with carnal pleasures which start off with a bubble bath or two.

The phone rings. It's mama wanting to know if she forgot to turn off the stove. On the way to the kitchen, girl stops off at the bathroom. Guy and girl start frolicking. Guy puts girl on shoulders and they set off, naked, to the kitchen.

They crash through the door, giggling, only to find themselves face to face with parents, family, friends, etc, who decided to surprise girl with surprise kitchen tea. Girl ends up in a mental home and guy is never heard from again.

This is the only version I have come across that includes the bathroom scene, and the only South African version that includes the 'punishment' at the end. The woman's mental collapse and the man's disappearance are standard features of the international versions of the legend, but seem not to have caught on in South Africa.

In the United States, the legend of the Nude Surprise Party is so prevalent, an entire book has been devoted to

136

variations on the plot. Professor William Hugh Jansen of the University of Kentucky published and compared no less than twenty-eight versions with widely divergent plots.

He collected his earliest 'piggyback' variety in 1959. It supposedly happened in Somerset, Kentucky and, as reprinted by Jan Brunvand, goes like this:

> There was a young couple of well-to-do families who were engaged to be married. On the girl's birthday, the two of them went out, but returned home rather early. Upon returning to the girl's home it was discovered that the parents were away. The two of them decided to do something 'different' and removed all their clothing. Soon thereafter, the telephone rang. When she answered it, the girl was asked by her mother to please go to the basement and turn off the automatic washer, which she had forgotten. When the conversation ended, one of the couple decided it would be fun if the boy carried the girl downstairs piggyback. This they proceeded to do, and when they reached the bottom of the stairs, the lights came on and a large group of friends and relatives yelled 'Surprise!' The girl, I was told, had a nervous breakdown and was institutionalised. The boy has neither been seen or heard of since.

It appears South Africans are made of sterner stuff. The local versions usually allow the couple to live with their folly, and each other. In versions where a vicar is part of the surprise reception, perhaps the couple does not appear in church for a while thereafter, but this does not especially ruin their lives.

As folklorists would have it, this possibly indicates a slip in our moral standards. The confrontation in the finale, which in many versions involves prominent members of the community, is, according to Brunvand in *The Vanishing Hitchhiker*, 'obviously symbolic of the irreconcilable clash between middle-aged upholders of traditional values and young people who no longer accept the old morality. The consistent lesson is that the old morality triumphs.' In the American versions, the licentious youngsters are harshly punished for their sins, but South Africans get off comparatively lightly.

This is a little surprising, as the repressive form of Calvinist morality that has shaped much of official South African thinking over the past few centuries should have had the couple burning in hellfire. On the other hand, this very morality perhaps dictates that merely being exposed in an immoral deed is punishment enough. Being committed to a lunatic asylum is as nothing compared to the censure of a conservative community.

The Man in the Superman Costume

The story of the couple involved in kinky sex and a Superman costume, with which this book opened, is one which has done the rounds all over the world.

This version cropped up in about 1986, and not long afterwards was the subject of an eager investigation by reporters at the *Star*. Somehow they had come to hear the story as something that had just happened. They enlisted the co-operation of all their contacts from pubs to police stations, from hospitals to costume shops, but did not find a shred of evidence.

Coincidentally, 1986 also saw the publication in the UK of *The Book of Nastier Legends* by Paul Smith. One of the legends was this one:

A slightly overweight middle-aged man was admitted to the emergency out-patients department of the local hospital one evening not so long ago. He had a broken ankle but, perhaps more surprisingly, was attired in a Superman costume. The staff were naturally very puzzled and persistently questioned him on what had happened. He was very reticent to tell them. Nevertheless, finally the story came out.

Neighbours in the well-to-do middle-class estate where he lived had heard cries coming from his home. As they could get no reply when they banged on the door, the emergency services were called. When the police broke in, they found the man's wife, stark naked and manacled, spreadeagled on the bed. The gentleman in question was in his Superman suit lying on the floor trapped under a wardrobe and unable to free himself.

Evidently in a wild sexual frenzy he had been going to jump off the top of the wardrobe onto his wife. Unfortunately, the wardrobe had fallen over, he had lost his balance, broken his ankle, and become trapped. It is said the ambulancemen were crying with laughter and unable to hold the stretcher steady as they carried him out of the house.

Smith commented in a footnote that 'This delightful story only surfaced in the UK this year.' Could it have been a response to the wave of media hype surrounding the relaunching of the Superman comic in 1986, or advance notice that the age of permissiveness was over — anyone trying anything kinky would pay for the crime? Or did it really happen to someone, somewhere?

This is the question Barry Ronge asked, tongue-in-cheek, in his Spit and Polish column in the *Sunday Times* magazine on 30 April 1989:

We all know that there is one particular Jo'burg hotel where security men are told to be circumspect about investigating sounds of lashing and moans of pain because these are just some specialised ladies of the night plying their masterful trade.

But one night the screams were so insistent that they did break the door down to find a young woman, stark naked save for high-heeled shoes, tied to the bed, screaming her head off.

They ran to help her but she directed them to the cupboard where they found a man dressed in a Batman suit, with two broken ankles. He had apparently been about to swoop down on his captive for a little kinky love play and had climbed onto a cupboard to do so, but his weight broke the cupboard and he fell through onto the floor and injured his feet.

The wardrobe was locked, he couldn't move and the girl was powerless because she was tied up, and so he found himself coming out of the closet in a more catastrophic sense then he had ever imagined.

I don't expect anyone to own up to that one, especially as he is supposed to have been quite a senior and well-known businessman, but perhaps you can think back to some prominent person who managed to have a skiing accident without going to Kitzbühel ...

The *Sunday Times*, having forgotten Ronge's column, gave it an equally topical twist in their 18 March 1990 issue:

BATMAN'S LOVE FLIGHT FALLS FLAT
Sunday Times Reporter, Frankfurt

A kinky husband had a crash-landing after dressing as Batman to make a 'flight of love' from the top of his wardrobe.

Ambulancemen found the man, identified as Willy K, spreadeagled on the floor with a broken arm and jaw.

The Batman costume covered only the top half of his body.

Willy's wife Helena, 31, could not help because she was tied to the bed.

Willy lay in agony for an hour. He was rescued after

the couple's screams alerted neighbours in Frankfurt, West Germany.

Helena said: 'He slipped.'

Willy was taken to hospital – still wearing the costume.

Two interesting points emerge from the story. Firstly, its origin in West Germany makes it practically uncheckable for a South African publication (the credit, *Sunday Times* Reporter, Frankfurt, is merely *Times* practice for foreign stories that don't carry a name byline and is likely to have been lifted from the British *Daily Mirror*, with which the *Sunday Times* has a reciprocal agreement for lifting rights.)

Secondly, and probably most fascinating from the folklorist's point of view, is the evolution of the costume from the old versions of the story to the two *Sunday Times* variations. After years of dressing up in Superman's red, white and blue, the sexual adventurer has suddenly donned Batman's grim black and purple garb.

Psychoanalysts would no doubt point out the relation of this development to the subconscious mind's reaction to the growing dangers of promiscuous sex — kinky or otherwise — as a result of Aids. It is easy to conclude that the spectre of death lurking about sex would transform a bright, 'pure' image in urban legends into one that is dark, menacing and merciless.

However, there is a simpler explanation. Until 1989, Superman was probably the best known hero in the costumed supermen's hall of fame. Then came one of the most commercially successful films of all time: *Batman*. The character had been around in comics for almost as long as Superman. However, it was only with the feature film, and the enormous media hype surrounding it, that Batman really came into his own as a major figure in the mass consciousness. The comic book itself was re-created as a dark, adult-oriented medium. It inspired several acclaimed 'graphic novels', the new comic form that is slowly earning literary respectability for comics.

And thus it was that the latest version of the story comes, allegedly, from one of the most genteel communities in the country: Hout Bay, a small enclave of village life in the bustling Cape Peninsula. The story is apparently set in about February 1990:

This family was just settling down to dinner when they heard loud screaming coming from next door. They all ran out to see what was happening. They thought someone had broken in and was attacking the young couple who lived there.

They banged on the door, but the screaming carried on. It was the woman, screaming, 'Help, help!'

So eventually the father of the family kicks down the door, and runs in. He follows the screams to the bedroom, and there he sees the young wife, spreadeagled and tied to the bedposts, naked.

Her husband is lying unconscious on the floor, and he's wearing a Batman costume.

It turns out he was going to leap onto her from the top of the wardrobe, but he misjudged, and hit the floor, breaking his leg and knocking himself out.

The message is: don't be kinky, kids.

13 ... BUT WERE AFRAID TO TRY

Urban legend law says that even when sex is not kinky, it must still be perilous. As the previous chapter showed, the wages of sin can be somewhat discouraging. Sometimes, though, they are also hilarious.

The Condoms and the Chemist

There is the classic legend about the young gentleman who is getting ready to go out on a blind date with a supposedly 'hot' young woman. He wants to be prepared for any eventuality and pops down the road to the chemist. The pharmacist seems to be an amiable sort of fellow, so the young man grins broadly at him, and tells him that he's certain to 'score' that night, so he wants to purchase the establishment's best condoms. That night he arrives at his date's house, and her father comes to the door. Surprise, surprise, it's the pharmacist.

Apparently the legend dates back to the 1940s and 1950s in the USA, when condoms were the preferred contraceptive, but caused enormous embarrassment for young men who had to buy them without anyone actually seeing what they were buying.

A favourite adolescent legend in South Africa in the 1960s and 1970s was the 'fact' that certain cafés were illegal stockists of condoms, which they kept under the counter.

The Bloemfontein outlet, at least in my school's neighbourhood, was known as the Bluegum Café. Due to some misdemeanour committed by a schoolboy there, the establishment was permanently out of bounds to the school's hostel boarders. Naturally, this merely strengthened the belief that the Bluegum was the source of all things strange and dangerous.

But that wasn't the urban legend. The legend was this: you could not actually go into one of these cafés and ask for condoms. What you did was go up to the counter, and take out a 20-cent coin. Making sure the proprietor was watching closely, you flipped the coin with one hand, caught it, and slapped it down on the counter. The proprietor would then take the coin, and hand you a pack of three condoms.

Neither myself nor anyone I know ever witnessed this ritual. Supposedly, it was designed to avoid the embarrassment of stating one's needs out loud. No one seemed to consider that this contrived performance might be even more embarrassing for a schoolboy than merely saying 'Rubbers, please.'

The purpose of the legend is fairly clear: firstly, it expresses the embarrassment faced by young men — certainly the embarrassment schoolboys would imagine themselves facing in that situation — who need to acquire condoms; secondly, it suggests an easy way out: you are saved from having to expose your activities verbally to a stranger, as long as you are able to give the code signal.

And then, of course, the whole ritual turns sex into a conspiracy which, when you are an adolescent, it most certainly is.

I have not encountered the coin-flipping story for years, although the chemist legend crops up from time to time. It, too, has taken a back seat, particularly when supermarkets began to take over the task of dispensing condoms.

Then came Aids, and massive international campaigns to promote 'safe sex' through the use of condoms. Suddenly, condoms are back at the forefront of sexual consciousness, and suddenly new versions of the legend are cropping up again. This one was sent to me by someone who heard it recently in Cape Town:

The Blind Date

A soccer team travelled from Johannesburg to Cape Town for a Saturday match. On arrival they were told blind dates had been arranged for them for the evening after the game. One player, practical minded, decided to plan ahead. Just in case his date was willing, he would be prepared. He went into a chemist's shop and bought some condoms from the attractive female assistant. That night, when he arrived at the party, he was introduced to his date. It was the chemist's assistant who had sold him the condoms.

There are many variations on this legend. Sometimes the plot moves ahead to the moment the young couple are already entwined in each other's bodies. For instance, there's the policeman who spots a young couple making love on the beach. He moves in for the kill, switches on his search beam, and shouts 'You're under arrest!' As the startled naked couple leap up, he recognises his own daughter.

To get an idea of the lengths this kind of variation can go to, here's a report from the 11 April 1990 edition of *People* magazine, South Africa's answer to the *National Enquirer*:

> When a police chief in a vice raid stripped away a sensuous beauty's mask, he couldn't believe his eyes. The sexy temptress was ... his own mother.
> 'Mother, is that really you?' he sobbed. 'Please tell me it's not you.' Then, as TV cameras rolled, he turned as red as the garters his 45-year-old mother flashed during her sexy striptease act at a businessman's club. Leading a highly publicised raid on the exclusive club, with

145

> *reporters and photographers in tow, the heartbroken cop*
> *had no choice but to clamp handcuffs on his mother and*
> *haul her off to jail.*

That in itself would make a classic urban legend. But there is more:

> *... the story didn't end there. In the audience that night*
> *was a powerful and respected federal judge ... none other*
> *than the police chief's dad. Judge Pable Mendoza, 52,*
> *was speechless when he realised the stripper he'd been*
> *drooling over was actually his wife. Even when the*
> *masked and scantily attired woman had sat on his lap, he*
> *had no idea she was the person he'd been married to for*
> *27 years.*
> *... The shocking headlines were hardly what Police*
> *Chief Jesus Mendoza had in mind when he declared war*
> *on pornography and drugs in Chalapa, Mexico.*
> *'The raid was supposed to gain him enough good*
> *publicity to launch a career in politics,' explained one of*
> *Chief Mendoza's advisers.*

The details of the story — names, places — suggest it may be true. However, I have been informed that the story was bought by *People* from the American supermarket tabloid, the *National Enquirer*. Its source in a medium that is openly more interested in sensational stories than hard news reporting makes it suspect, especially considering the wealth of typical urban legend ingredients.

There is the theme of the tables turned, twice; of the moral authority figure who discovers that the morals he is assigned to defend have broken down within the very bosom of his family; of the sexually curious male (the judge plays the same role as the man who goes to the chemist) who made an unfortunate choice of establishment at which to spend his money; of the authority figure who is

146

appropriately punished for abusing his authority; and finally, of the wayward wife and mother whose transgressions are exposed in the most public, embarrassing manner possible.

If it isn't an urban legend, it should be.

The Severed Nipple

Many of the caught-in-the-act legends are set at beaches and drive-ins. In one version, the small-town police chief pays a visit to the local drive-in to make sure no hanky-panky is going on. During his torchlight patrol he comes across a car with seriously steamed up windows. He wrenches open the door ... and his own daughter, in a state of undress, tumbles out.

This story seems to have had its origin in the 1950s and 1960s, when drive-ins had come into their own in the USA. The places came to be known as 'passion pits', because of the golden opportunity they provided for 'making out'.

Police regularly claimed to have 'cleaned up' these places, so that they would be safe for families again. Of course, they could hardly keep all those teenage hormones under guard, so drive-in passion survived, and so did the urban legends surrounding it.

There is a rather gruesome variation on the theme. One correspondent introduced his version with the information that 'This story has been told to me as being absolutely true ...' Strangely enough, as I was told it by different people, it really happened at four different drive-in cinemas on the Reef, one in Durban, one in East London, one in Cape Town.

A couple were 'making out' in a car at a drive-in cinema. The young man got so excited that he accidentally bit the nipple off the girl's breast. Screaming and bleeding, still naked, the girl leaped from the car and ran between the parked cars until she collapsed and died from loss of blood.

While that is not especially kinky, the punishment is most cruel and unusual. It sounds so over-the-top, it almost violates urban legends' own unwritten rules of moral justice. However, further examination reveals a possible reason.

According to one informant, who was a teenager in the 1950s, the event occurred at a time when drive-in fooling around was the only sexual outlet for young people. Of course, it was heavily censured behaviour, and serious repercussions were predicted by the moral guardians of the time. To this particular informant, however, none of this was relevant.

You see, he knew the woman to whom it had happened. She had survived the experience and supposedly used to tell people about it as if it were a great joke. As a result, the story spread, and developed into an urban legend containing ghastly consequences.

My informant supplied me with the name of the victim and the area where she resides today. He assured me that she was a good sport and would tell me the full story. Hot on the trail of cracking an urban legend wide open, I tracked down the woman's phone number, and called her.

The phone was indeed answered by the lady in question. Unfortunately, she said she knew nothing of the story, and had never heard of anything remotely like it.

Perhaps it never did happen, perhaps she had forgotten, perhaps she had wanted to forget. Whatever the case, another urban legend survives intact.

However, it also leaves the question of the cruel and unusual punishment hanging in the air. Perhaps this was in fact how the legend had begun, with a real but non-fatal event, which then developed into the version with the terrible fate.

Perhaps urban legends sometimes reserve such punishment for minor misdemeanours as a warning to the rest of us: don't even *think* about transgressing the moral rules around here, kid.

Indeed, just thinking about such things holds its risks in urban legend country. Especially if you project your own hidden fears into other people's motives. For instance, here, as told by Barry Ronge in his Spit and Polish column in the *Sunday Times* magazine, 4 June 1989, is the tale of ...

The Nervous Hairdresser

Just at closing time in an almost deserted shopping mall, the sole hairdresser left on duty in the shop hears a knock at the door and outside she sees a handsome but rather distraught young man. He begs forgiveness for arriving so late but he is from out of town on an important business trip, his day has gone wrong on him and the haircut he wanted to have just could not be fitted in. He has a crucial business dinner that night, he needs to look his best, so won't she please take pity on him and please, please cut his hair. He will even pay double the price for overtime. His hair is a bit shaggy, he has a nice honest face so against her better judgement she lets him in. Yes, she has read those Rape Crisis handouts about not letting strange men in ... but the guy seems genuine, doesn't he? She goes to the back to collect the towels and the plastic cover. Just before she goes back she takes one more nervous look in the mirror to make sure no one has followed him in. She sees a reflection of the man from behind and what she sees makes her blood run cold. He has his hands in his lap in front of him, and one elbow is sticking out at the side as it makes regular rubbing movements ... She makes the obvious deduction, picks up an enormous bottle of conditioner, runs up behind him, knocks him out of the chair with it and rushes out of the shop screaming for help. She comes back with security guards, cops and passers-by who see the guy on the floor, out cold, his zip still done up, and his spectacles, which he was quite innocently polishing with the tail of his shirt which he had pulled out of his trousers, broken on the floor.

Ronge says he first heard the story from a hairdresser's assistant in Randburg, who told him it had actually happened to her boss. A year later a Cape Town hairdresser told a luridly embellished version at a lunch party.

If it's not a true story, he says, it ought to be. 'I cannot think of more adequate a metaphor for modern life than that,' he says. He speculates that urban legends are perhaps 'a form of collective anxiety which we project outwards and which has become the true public theatre of our times'. They externalise all our silliest anxieties about status, class and being made to look ridiculous.

In that vein, we could include this old favourite, as told by Gus Silber in *Style*'s August 1987 edition:

The Flirt that Hurt

On her way home from the hairdresser, the lacquered lady sees her husband's legs sticking out from under the chassis of his beloved Ford Cortina. She tiptoes up the driveway, reaches out in silence, unzips her husband's fly, jiggles, and runs giggling into the house. The first thing she sees is her husband, lazily reading a newspaper in the lounge. Her mouth falls open: 'But ... I thought you ... oh, no, then who is... a friend of yours? Your MECHANIC?' Husband and wife rush to the Cortina, under which there is no sign of movement. They extract the mechanic: there is a deep gash where he bumped his head, and a pool of dark, oily blood all around. He survives. He never forgets.

The legend, well-known in the United States, is part of a rich tradition of women — particularly wives — behaving in an untoward manner and suffering the consequences. The next tale fits even more blatantly into this mould.

The Nude in the Laundry

America's favourite advice columnist, Ann Landers, in 1975 reported that the letter she had published with the single best response in twenty years had been from a woman who liked doing her housework in the nude. Five years later, she was still getting responses to this letter, including a story which the correspondent claimed to be a summary of a 'news item':

> *An Ohio housewife was doing her laundry in the basement when she impulsively decided to take off her soiled house-dress and put it in the machine. Her hair was in rollers and the pipes overhead were leaking. She spotted her son's football helmet and put it on her head. There she was, stark naked (except for the football helmet), when she heard a cough. The woman turned around and found herself staring into the face of the meter reader. As he headed for the door, his only comment was, 'I hope your team wins, lady.'*

Jan Brunvand reports numerous versions of this story. One has the woman putting her dress in the washing machine because she wants to make up a full load and, after putting on the helmet, is surprised by the plumber whom her husband had called to fix those leaking pipes. In effect, the plumber is the husband's moral spy, indirectly checking up on her indiscretions.

I have yet to come across a South African version of this legend. Perhaps it is because few South African homes have functional basements. Perhaps the football helmet, an item alien to South African sport, is an essential ingredient.

Nevertheless, the experience of being caught in the nude remains a powerful theme in local urban legends.

Not entirely coincidentally, it is also regarded as a common dream experience. Dreaming that you suddenly find yourself naked in a crowd of people, or in the middle of a bustling supermarket or in a busy street without a stitch of clothing, is as 'popular' as dreams of flying and falling. Naturally, the element of subconscious fear that operates in these dreams is a powerful motivator of urban legends.

Like the nude dreams, however, the legends are generally harmless. Acute embarrassment is about the worst fate that befalls the victims.

There are indications that such legends may be giving way to stories that are more crude and bizarre, and more adequately reflect the traumas that have come to be associated with sex in the 1990s.

14 WELCOME TO THE WORLD OF AIDS

Most urban legends about Aids fall into two categories: those that are little more than jokes, and those that are full-blown conspiracy theories. However, the manner in which the latter have been spread in South Africa makes them a worthy topic of an urban legends investigation. These are ominous legends that are taken seriously by many otherwise intelligent people.

But first, the 'jokes'.

The Message in a Coffin

A girl decides to go overseas for a year, to recover from a broken heart. Overseas, probably in France, she meets Mr Right. It's LOVE in a big way and they move in together. Before long, they decide to get married. She comes back to South Africa to break the news to her parents. At the airport, loverboy gives her a beautifully wrapped going-away gift. She's told not to open it until she's on the aeroplane. Tearfully, missing him already, she opens the gift as the plane takes off. Inside is an empty box shaped like a coffin. In the box is a note. It says: 'Welcome to the Aids Club.'

I have heard numerous versions of this story, and for some reason most of them have the girl meeting the man in England. In some cases, she has to promise to open the gift only once she has landed back in South Africa. Her parents come to fetch her at the airport, and she opens the gift in front of them.

153

Do not think, however, that this cautionary tale is aimed only at women. There is a male counterpart, as told by this correspondent:

> *This is probably just bar talk. It's a story about a woman who becomes very promiscuous and sleeps around. She picks men up in clubs and places, and then goes home with them for the night. The man wakes up the next morning and she's gone. He walks into the bathroom and there, written in red lipstick on the mirror, it says: 'Welcome to the world of Aids.'*

So much for light relief. The next legend has its source in the very real world of South African racial intolerance.

Antibodies Are Your Friends

Let us return to the pamphlet discussed in Chapter 2. The 'AMANDLA!' pamphlet, calling on blacks to rise up and kill all whites on 10 April 1990, included not only that call to blacks to rise up, but also an 'article' headed 'THE AIDS VIRUS IS A RACIST PLOT'. That section of the pamphlet, credited to one Philemon Ndladla, read, in full:

> *How much do you and your family know about the Aids virus? Did you know that FW de Klerk and his racist white government chose the Aids virus to chase us out of our Azania?*
>
> *Israel developed the virus!*
>
> *The scientists at the Tel Aviv University of Biological Studies invented the disease to use against our friends in the PLO, but the racist South Africans paid doctor Cecil Roth and his team a BILLION Rands to give the South Africans the virus to use against us. PW Botha and his racist friends in the CP and AWB distributed the virus since 1986, and since then our brothers and sisters*

*fighting for freedom from the white racist oppressors
have been dying.*

What can we do?

*It was scientifically proven by Doctor Ruben Sher that
Indian, and NOT white women have the antibody to the
Aids virus. The white racists started a slander campaign
so that we wouldn't find a cure, but our friends in the DP
found out that to stop us EVER catching Aids, all we
have to do is to have sex with an Indian woman. I have
already made sure about being Aids free so that I can
have lots of kids.*

HAVE YOU?

If ever there has been a more crude and offensive attempt at
stirring up racial hatred, I haven't seen it. The pamphlet
aims at inciting racial discord between virtually every ethnic
group in South Africa. Only extremely ignorant or badly
misinformed people could begin to take it seriously.

However, the fabric of this distortion was largely
overlooked in the light of the death call elsewhere on the
pamphlet.

The most obvious flaw in the argument is the writer's
confusion of antibodies — which reveal the presence of the
disease — with immunity to the disease. Beside this myth,
there are three folkloristic elements to the pamphlet:
* Scientists invented the Aids virus.
* Aids is a racist plot.
* Sex with an Indian woman provides immunity to Aids.

The only detail in the pamphlet that relates to reality is the
fact that Ruben Sher really is a doctor, and really is involved
with Aids research. In fact, he is head of the Aids Centre at
the SA Institute for Medical Research. His response was
quoted by the *Star* of 10 April 1990.

Sher described the pamphlet as 'a tissue of lies from
beginning to end and not based on any scientific or medical

facts'.

He said 'he had decided to react to the pamphlet because he had received dozens of telephone calls from distressed people'.

Sher released the following statement:

> *The fact that a person has antibodies to the virus indicates the person is indeed infected with the virus, is infectious and can pass on the virus to others during sexual contact. To say the only way to protect against becoming infected is to have sexual relations with a person who has antibodies is completely incorrect and dangerous.*

Perhaps that in itself is a clue. Perhaps the perpetrators were hoping to help spread Aids among blacks, and at the same time create racial friction between blacks and Indians, through their crude disinformation campaign.

Sher commented: 'It is my opinion that the ANC would not stoop so low as to publish such racist filth.'

The ANC, in the person of deputy president Nelson Mandela himself, dissociated themselves from the pamphlet, and the SA Police backed them up, describing it as an amateurish fake.

Ironically, the pamphlet does have a vague basis — but it is a basis set purely in urban legend. In late 1989 a myth emerged in the Durban area — which has a high Indian and Zulu population — that Indian women carried natural Aids antibodies. The details of the myth suggested that the word 'anti' had created confusion and was interpreted as meaning it conferred immunity upon these women. Anyone who had sex with them, it was said, would have this immunity passed on to them.

The legend circulated largely in the townships, but clearly served the purposes of white supremacist propaganda as well as it did the elements of racial intolerance that sometimes arises between blacks and Indians. It functions on precisely the same level as many myths that intolerant whites believe about blacks and their genetic makeup.

The antibody urban legend, as with many of the kidnap legends, masks its racism behind the façade of an anecdote, story or narrative.

The same applies to the myth (legend?) that Aids is a white racist plot to wipe out blacks. It is hardly surprising that blacks might want to believe whites want to wipe them out — a fairly vocal sector of the far right has threatened to do just that.

And when one considers the cold, calculated thinking that went into the conception and execution of apartheid, a myth about a 'racist disease' has a certain ring of truth about it.

In this light, let us look at another pamphlet which appeared early in 1990. It emerged at about the same time as the first pamphlet, and carried suspicious parallels. It was tucked under windscreen wipers on vehicles parked in the streets of conservative white towns on the West Rand, rather than being faxed to businesses on the Reef as was the other pamphlet. Roger Makings reported the following details in the *Sunday Times* of 15 April 1990:

> ... *the pamphlets warn whites against visiting:*
> * *Multiracial hotels, restaurants and churches;*
> * *Swimming pools, spa baths, beaches and public toilets;*
> * *Salad bars, discos, public bars;*
> * *Churches where 'common communion cups' are used.*
> *The pamphlet was compiled by a mysterious organisation calling itself the AIDS Information Distributing Society of SA.*
> *It also urges employers of black domestic servants to subject them to monthly blood tests to 'safeguard your family'.*

> *The pamphlet concludes: 'If you have any love for your family, children and friends please make a photostat and hand to everyone you come in contact with to save the white race from extinction.'*

It sounds like the flipside of the document aimed at blacks, only this time shifting responsibility for spreading Aids to blacks, and raising just about every myth yet devised about the disease.

Ruben Sher again responded:

> *I have never in my life read such rubbish. The only way anyone will get Aids from an infected servant is through having sex. And to suggest that the virus can be spread through coughing, sneezing, dry kissing, tears, sweat and mosquitoes is nothing but right-wing propaganda.*
>
> *There have been no recorded cases of celibates, elderly sexually inactive people, happily married couples or children between the ages of two and 20 getting the virus casually.*

So much for the myths about how Aids is spread. It is debatable whether these could be classified as urban legends. They are more closely related to schoolyard myths of the type that warn of catching diseases from toilet seats. There is no narrative, or story line, attached to these myths, which suggests that they may be at an early stage of urban legend development.

However, one fully grown urban legend has emerged from all this misinformation.

It appears to date from almost precisely the time that the pamphlets were reported, ie April 1990. I first heard this legend at the beginning of July 1990, and was told it was something that had 'happened' about two months previously.

158

Beware of Maids

A well-to-do-couple in Durban noticed that their baby was very lethargic and it got sick quite easily. Finally, they took it to a doctor for tests. He ran test after test after test, and finally came to the terrible conclusion: the baby had Aids. The couple couldn't believe it, but they started investigating. In the course of their investigations they had their maid tested — and found she also had Aids. It turned out that the maid had got the disease from her boyfriend and, while looking after her employers' baby, she would breastfeed the child herself. As a result, she had infected the child with the disease.

Besides being a fleshed out version of one of the Aids fallacies apparently spread by rightwingers, the story has all the characteristics of an urban legend, with themes ranging from racial intolerance to an enemy within to a mystery solved. Its most fascinating aspect is the powerful metaphor it provides of white fear for the future: the child is fed on a diet of a black woman's milk, and for that it pays the ultimate price. The legend seems to symbolise a fear that integration will lead to the death of white culture/values/civilisation.

The AIDS Conspiracy

There are many grand conspiracy theories. On the same day the *Sunday Times* reported the 'beware of maids' pamphlet, *City Press* carried a lengthy report headed 'AIDS MYTH EXPOSED!', a story reprinted from *New African* magazine. At a glance, it seemed it was going to be a timely exposé of all the pamphlets floating about. Sadly, it wasn't. It began thus:

> *The myth that Aids began in Africa has been exposed as a fallacy. In fact, it started in America. The new evidence comes from a sensational documentary by German film-makers Heino Claassen and Molte Rauch.*
>
> *... Providing solid scientific evidence, the film shows that Africa was vilified, by top scientists and the media, on doubtful evidence.*

The feature then traces a history of disinformation on how Aids was alleged to have begun in Africa and spread to the West, whereas all evidence seemed to point to a North American origin.

So far so good; these are all points of debate in ongoing discussions about Aids. But then:

> *... why has so much time, energy, money and misinformation been put about to portray Africa as the villain of the Aids drama? Is there a sinister motive? Jacob Segal* (referred to earlier in the report as forming with his wife Lili 'one of the world's most formidable biological, virological teams') *thinks there is.*
>
> *He believes the Aids virus is man-made and that a great deal of effort has gone into covering up this fact ...*
>
> *According to Segal, the Aids virus has been recombined from the Visna virus, which causes a deadly brain disease in sheep and goats, and a piece of the leukemia virus. He believes that human beings, probably prisoners, were experimented on and did not show much effect except for a short, influenza-like infection.*
>
> *The 'guinea-pigs' were then released but, unknown to anyone at the time, they carried with them the original Aids virus.*
>
> *A number of scientists have strongly refuted this theory, but say the Aids virus could have been the result of an accident in gene technology or microbiology ...*
>
> *Could the laboratory viruses have accidentally escaped or been stolen? It seems very probable. In an*

*area of Fort Detrick, the Pentagon's centre for chemical
and biological research, a quart of the highly dangerous
Chicungungya virus vanished. According to experts, that
amount is sufficient to wipe out a major part of mankind.*

*In 1969, the United States Department of Defence
asked a Congress committee to allocate $10-million for
research to produce an artificial virus which could
destroy the human immune system. According to the
Pentagon spokesman at the committee meeting,
consultations with outstanding scientists had already
been held. All further details were declared secret.*

There is one small problem with all this evidence. It was first
trotted out by East Germans in 1989, before the Wall came
tumbling down, and while the propaganda war between
East and West was still raging. The Soviet Union, via its
official media, had also claimed that Aids had been created
in American laboratories.

Some of the claims even suggested it had been designed to
wipe out blacks. The crudity of the propaganda ensured
that it earned little credibility beyond the Iron Curtain.
Since the winding down of the Cold War, and with glasnost
bearing fruit in Eastern Europe, the propagandists have
fallen silent.

However, the belated publication of this material in *City
Press* drew an angry response from the American Embassy
in Pretoria. Kent Obee, Counsellor for Public Affairs, wrote
a letter to the newspaper:

> *The article is based on a 1989 West German film 'Aids:
> The African Legend'. This film and the New African
> article repeat the totally false claims of the East German
> researcher Jacob Segal. Jacob and Lili Segal are not
> '... one of the world's most formidable biological teams'.
> In fact, their research is scandalously shoddy.*
>
> *The article repeats Segal's theory that Aids was*

manufactured by combining the Visna virus with a leukemia virus. No serious scientist believes this. There are no similarities between the Aids virus and the Visna and bovine leukemia viruses when genetic sequences are examined.

The world's scientific and medical communities have rejected the Segals' absurd theory that Aids was created artificially ... The world's top medical authorities have repeatedly stated that attempts to blame it on anyone – the Americans, the Africans, or anyone else – are not only absurd but also distract us from the real challenge – the task of finding a cure for this horrible disease.

City Press was apparently sufficiently abashed to run the letter on 29 April 1990 under a large headline, 'AIDS STORY PROVED TO BE NONSENSE'.

The truly fascinating point about all this is the myths that surround the myths that have evolved about Aids. This is clearly a growth area for urban legends.

Unlike many older sex-related legends, whose origins are lost in time and retelling, Aids legends can only date from the early 1980s onward. Its recent origin — or identification — means that folklorists may actually be able to monitor the emergence and development of the legends.

It does not mean that they would be able to pinpoint exact sources or origins, but they may better be able to interpret the meanings, relevance and function of these legends.

For now, suffice it to say that the virus remains a mysterious, threatening and terminal disease, and its dark menace as well as its 'secret' origins are likely to be reflected in the myths and legends that continue to grow around Aids.

15 LEGENDARY CROOKS

As much as we may value justice, we cannot fail to admire the thieves of our times. They bring to their profession an unmatchable level of inventiveness. Just the other day, cousins of a friend of mine arrived home from work and ... er, wait a minute, it was my friend's mother-in-law's best friend's cousin ... or something. Anyway, the story goes like this:

The Thoughtful Thieves

A young married couple arrives home after a tough day's commuting to and from work by train and bus. To their absolute dismay, their treasured little car, their pride and joy, is missing from their driveway. They are terribly shocked — this was such a peaceful neighbourhood, the house was such a good investment for their future family.

They report the theft to the police, and go to bed miserable that night. Next morning they wake up, and the husband goes to open the bedroom curtains. And what does he see, but their car, parked in the street outside.

He rushes out in his pyjamas. The car seems to be in perfect shape. Then he sees a note stuck under the windscreen wipers. It reads: 'Please accept our apologies — we had an emergency and just had to borrow a car. To prove it was in good faith, and to compensate, we've attached two theatre tickets for tonight. Enjoy the play!'

Sure enough, two tickets are attached. The couple's faith in human nature is restored, not to mention their faith in the investment value of their carefully furnished home. That night they go to the theatre, enjoy themselves thoroughly, and make their languid way home.

Only to find, their home has been entirely cleaned out by burglars!

This is one of those legends that ruins dinner parties. There is bound to be at least one person present who knows someone who has actually experienced something like this. Well... he doesn't know them personally — it happened to the parents of his girlfriend's neighbours. And so on. To date, I have the names of about a dozen friends of friends to whom this supposedly happened, and have followed up several leads with absolutely no results ('Yes, it did happen, but not to us. It was the chap across the street, but he moved out three months ago ...').

Another version sends the victims to a ballet performance. It mentions Johannesburg specifically as the home of the victims, the State Theatre in Pretoria as the venue of the ballet (a 50km trip, giving the burglars more time to ply their trade), and even *Swan Lake* as the ballet.

An article on 'fertile yarns' by Jaap Boekkooi in the *Sunday Star* on 7 July 1987 mentions the legend almost dismissively. In this instance, the couple are about to leave for the theatre when they find their car has been stolen. Several days later it is returned, tickets under the wiper. The legend is referred to as an old story with a 'juicy French thriller twist'.

Writers of French thrillers may not be too impressed with the comparison, but the story remains compelling, popular and easily believed. One informant, who has a brother in the diplomatic service, insists that it was a stunt pulled by burglars in Buenos Aires.

An inevitable new South African variation draws on the joint evils of sports madness and junk mail:

A keen rugby fan, whose wife and son are also mad about the game, gets a letter in the post from some corporation he's never heard of. It tells him he's been selected as part of a special promotion to publicise the company and its public spiritedness.

Enclosed are three tickets to a major rugby match taking place in two weeks' time. He is delighted, as the tickets cost a fortune, and this allows him to take his wife as well as his son. Comes the day, the family troops off to the game. They have the time of their lives, and wend their way home after the game, weary but content — until they open the front door, and find the house has been ransacked.

While putting the finishing touches to this book, I received an excited phonecall from a friend who had just overheard the story being told on the bus. The narrator was a middle-aged woman who was recounting it as a personal experience:

'One day there was a knock at the door and there was a man who wanted to use the phone. His car was stuck, and he was late for a meeting, and he just had to phone and let them know. He looked respectable, but I wasn't taking any chances, and I refused.

'He begged me, and eventually I put the phone on an extension cord and passed it to him through the security gate. When he was finished he said he would repay me, and I said don't be silly, it's just a phonecall. He insisted, and said he'd be back the next day.

'Now I was really worried, because he had my address, my phone number and everything. I wondered what he had up his sleeve. The next day he actually came back, and he gave me two tickets for a show for that Saturday night. I can't remember what we saw, but it was something my sister and I — she lives with me — had been dying to see.

'But you know, the funniest thing happened. When we

165

got back that Saturday night, someone had broken into our house. They'd stolen the TV and all the appliances.'

My friend did not have the nerve to ask the woman for a phone number so that I could follow up the story. However, having heard me tell the story on several occasions, she listened intently to see how the woman told this one. Apparently, she was totally deadpan, and spoke in a sincere voice. And she didn't make a direct link between the burglary and the tickets, seeing them as two unusual, but separate experiences.

The tale was told on a bus in Johannesburg on 18 July 1990. Strangely enough, it came just a week after I first heard a version of the tickets being handed over at the door. In that version, the man had desperately needed to use the toilet: he had been doubled over with pain when the occupant went to answer his knock at the door. So grateful was the man for his relief, he brought a pair of tickets round the next day. And kindly burgled the home that night.

You just can't trust people these days. In your home, in your neighbourhood ... or in your friendly neighbourhood shopping mall. A variation on the decoy tickets ties in with a long tradition of shopping mall restroom legends. Instead of the usual mutilation or kidnapping, however, this one seems, at first, to concern a petty thief.

The Bag Snatcher in the Restroom

A woman from Boksburg shopping at Eastgate (in eastern Johannesburg) visited the ladies' restroom during the course of the morning. She went into a toilet stall, sat down, and leaned her bag against the wall of the stall.

Suddenly a hand reached under the dividing wall from the next stall, grabbed the bag and pulled it out of sight.

166

The woman quickly straightened her clothes and dashed out, but there was no sign of the bag snatcher. She went to Eastgate security to report the theft, and they said they would notify her if anything turned up.

The next day, she received a call from a man saying her bag had been found. Everything was intact, except her purse, which was missing. She was only too happy to get her ID book back, house keys and her credit cards. She'd come and collect her bag immediately.

Off to Eastgate she went, and went up to the security office to reclaim her handbag. When she got there the guards on duty had no record of the bag being recovered, and there was no entry in their logbook concerning the phonecall. A senior officer was called, but he also knew nothing about it.

Perplexed, the woman returned home — to find her house picked clean by burglars.

Fortunately, in real life, as in urban legends, the crooks do not always come off best.

The Chicken in the Hat

One of the oldest urban legends has a woman fainting at a supermarket check-out. Lately it has been happening at Checkers, and it is usually either an old white woman or a large black woman. A doctor is called, and hypothermia — exposure — is diagnosed. He is about to summon an ambulance when the woman's hat falls off and a frozen chicken rolls off her head.

Paul Smith, in *The Book of Nastier Legends*, tells an especially grisly British version, involving an old lady wearing a heavy coat, who dies of hypothermia.

You do not have to search very far to find a seminal version of this legend. Mark Twain used a variation in *The*

Adventures of Huckleberry Finn. Huck at one point steals a slab of butter he intends sneaking into a makeshift gaol holding Jim, the recaptured runaway slave. The butter is concealed beneath Huck's hat. Unfortunately, Tom Sawyer's family delays Huck, and the butter starts melting. The family spots the yellow ooze dripping down his face and an immediate diagnosis — brain fever — is made. As in the modern legend, though, the deception is quickly discovered.

Frozen butter or chicken is not usually the stuff of which urban legends are made. They are far too unthreatening, have far too little resonance in the subconscious. Modern folklore demands cars, large sums of money, or dead grand-mothers ...

The Deadly Crime

Jaap Boekkooi recounted this colloquial version of a popular South African legend in the *Sunday Star* of 7 July 1987:

> It concerns Mr X whose brand new Merc was swiped. He told the cops they mustn't worry, hey, for they're sure to find the car the next day. Y'see, he'd kept a bottle of poisoned mampoer on the backseat as an 'anti-theft device'. And sure, next day the fuzz sommer found the car, now a hearse, with three thieves inside, all stone dead.

Boekkooi recalled that some hopeful editor with jumbo headline fantasies asked him to check the tale, which had been reprinted in an insurance magazine. He spoke to numerous people who had heard the story from aunts, nephews, sister-in-laws' former boyfriends, and so on.

One version of the legend has also been told with an

added punchline: the car owner is charged with manslaughter, as law requires that you have to label a bottle clearly, 'Poison', if that is what you have put in it. The car owner is a prominent businessman, and even as we speak he is facing trial.

In the *Sunday Star* article, Boekkooi also says he's 'damn well not going to tell you about the Sun City stolen car story a second time ...' So I will have to tell it:

The Stolen Jackpot

A Johannesburg man discovers his brand new car has been stolen. He is dismayed, but not nearly as dismayed as his wife and kids, who had been looking forward to a trip to Sun City, the gambling mecca of South Africa. To make up for the loss, he borrows a car and they make the trip after all.

They arrive at Sun City and park in the huge lot outside the complex. Walking to the hyper-rail shuttle, he suddenly spots a dead ringer for his stolen car. The markings are the same. Even the numberplate is the same.

It just so happens that he still has his car keys with him. He tries the key in the door, and it opens. The whole family piles into the car, prodding here, checking there, to see if the car is intact. Someone opens the cubbyhole, and out pours R100 000 in R50 notes: the car thief's jackpot winnings!

Boekkooi refuses to repeat the story because 'if I do it wasn't Sun City but some other Sol place. Like Wild Coast Casino. Or Thaba Nchu. Or Thohoyandou. Any homeland or casino will do.' His prediction came true somewhat publicly three years later. The *Sunday Times*, always a reliable conduit of urban-legends-as-news, allowed columnist Tom Cobbleigh to get away with this report in the *Times* Diary on 6 May 1990:

When a Durban woman had her new car stolen with a boot full of meat recently she was distraught. But her husband was sympathetic and took her away for a day's outing to the Wild Coast Sun.

On their arrival she spotted her car in the car park. Her husband used his spare key and drove the car back to Durban. Back home they cleared the boot of the rotting meat and, on closer investigation, found R2 000 cash in the cubbyhole – obviously a gambling win of the thief.

They have now changed the registration number of their vehicle.

The Black Mafia

Those who are not too well disposed to 'casino homelands' will be pleased to learn that you do not have to go gambling to retrieve stolen cars. There is a quick, efficient service available in Johannesburg. This is the way I reported it in the *Weekly Mail* of 8 December 1989:

This story really did happen to a friend of a friend. Being a typical Johannesburg motorist, the time finally arrived for her car to be stolen. Now this was a rather old, reliable model with no insurance value. Recounting her woes, this friend of a friend said she'd do anything to get her car back. One of her colleagues murmured: 'Anything?' She nodded, and her colleague disappeared to make a phonecall. Two hours later the car was parked outside the office. Her delight was only slightly sullied when her colleague murmured that she now owed a favour to the 'black Mafia'.

The first half of the story really did happen. The victim was my secretary at the time. Her colleague suggested that the 'black Mafia' could return her car for a small fee. However, all attempts to contact a 'branch office' failed. Legend has it that Jay Naidoo, president of the Council of South African Trade Unions, had a similar experience when his car was stolen. Word went out that this was a hero of the Struggle, who should really not be deprived of transport. Within hours, his car was returned.

An American variation, as recounted by Jan Brunvand in *The Mexican Pet*, tells of a young couple in a wealthy suburb of some American city. They have quiet neighbours who are rumoured to have Mafia ties. One weekend their home is broken into, and numerous valuables are stolen. They ask the neighbour if he saw anything suspicious. He hadn't, but suggests they not report the crime immediately. He advises them to go to bed, and says he'll make a few phonecalls. Next day, all the valuables miraculously appear piled up on the couple's front porch.

Somehow, the thief is never caught in these legends. To help restore the balance of justice, then, here's a shocker that usually surfaces when a wedding or some other celebration is being discussed:

The Thief at the Wedding

A young Jewish couple get married and their parents throw a lavish reception in a Johannesburg catering hall. At the end of the party, the father of the bride picks up his jacket so that he can get his wallet out and pay the manager — the deal had been that he would settle the account at the end of the function, in cash. He had drawn the money from the bank a few days earlier, and had brought it in his wallet. Now he discovers that his wallet is missing!

After a frantic search there is still no sign of the money. The manager refuses to take a cheque or credit card. There is much explaining and embarrassment, and finally a hat is passed round to raise the money.

All's well that ends well.

Then, a few weeks later, after the video of the wedding has been edited, both families get together to relive the big day. Lo and behold, there on video, in crisp colour for all to see, is the father of the groom slipping a wallet out of the other father's jacket pocket. Words are exchanged, followed by punches, tears, bitter recriminations and, ultimately, divorce proceedings.

This is an enormously popular South African legend. It is often specifically Jewish in context — probably because of a tradition of paying in cash for the catering after a Jewish wedding.

In his second book, *The Choking Doberman*, Brunvand also reports a Jewish version, published in the New York *Jewish Week* in 1982. The father ends up paying by cheque, but is inconvenienced and embarrassed. After the exposé, the wedding is annulled. The newspaper insisted it really happened in the New York area that year.

In 1983 the Chicago *Sun-Times* reported a similar story, but without reference to any religious affiliation. The sum stolen is $20 000. The victim sends a copy of the videotape to the culprit, and a few days later the money is returned and no more is said. The *Sun-Times* lifted the story from the magazine *North Shore*, whose writer 'takes an oath it's the gospel truth'.

My personal favourite is the version told by Barry Ronge ('another wedding story which I suspect is also an apocryphal urban legend but it is so delicious it can be told again') in his Spit and Polish column in the *Sunday Times* Magazine of 30 April 1989. For once in an urban legend, it really does seem that the victims actually deserve their come-uppance:

The wedding was yet another posh affair where the families

172

were determined to outdo each other with expenditure on the spoiled bridal pair. The reception was in full swing.

The bride's father was beaming with pride and he had only still to pay the band, for which he had an envelope full of money (the band had given him a reduced rate for cash payment) and he had added R200 just in case he wanted the band to play longer.

His wife, a shrewd businesswoman, advised him not to pay the band too soon, for fear they would leave as soon as they had their money. He put the envelope in his jacket pocket.

As the evening grew rowdier, the liquor flowed and the room became hot. Papa put his jacket over the back of his chair and when he came back an hour later to fetch the money, it was, predictably, missing.

There was much searching and recrimination but in a room full of strangers milling about, who could he blame? He appeased the band and wrote it off to experience (and probably to tax as well. He had that kind of accountant).

The whole business was almost forgotten until the kids came back from Mauritius and the family sat down to see the wedding video which had been made by a live crew who roamed freely round the room all night.

At a certain moment Papa let out a yell, hit the rewind button and then the pause button to reveal the culprit in the background, in the act of stealing the money. It was, needless to say, the bridegroom's father calmly pocketing the cash.

Jan Brunvand is inclined to the 'cautionary tale' interpretation of such urban legends: stories with dark morals and warnings that are ignored at great risk. In an afterword to *The Vanishing Hitchhiker*, he writes: 'Time and again the meanings of stories are clear: "He should have known better,"; "She got what she deserved," etc.'

Indeed, he took the title of one of his books from a chilling example of this brand of legend: *The Choking Doberman*. In South Africa, the story is told by whites — usually with passionate conviction — as:

The Choking Rottweiler

A young woman lives by herself — against her parents' wishes — in an apartment in Johannesburg. She keeps a large Rottweiler for protection, leaving it in the flat while she's at work, and taking it for walks in the park at dusk. One night she gets home and is surprised when no dog bounds up to greet her when she opens the front door.

She steps in, switches on the light and sees her dog lying on the hallway carpet, choking on something. She can't get it to open its mouth, so, with the strength born of panic, she picks it up and carries it to her car.

She speeds to the vet, and begs him to see what is wrong with the dog. She tells him she left her front door open in her panic, so she must rush back. She leaves him her phone number and races home. As she gets to her front door, she hears the phone ring in her hallway. She dashes in and picks up the receiver. It is the vet.

He tells her to get out of her flat as fast as possible. 'Don't argue, just do it!' he urges.

Confused and anxious, she dashes out again, and then hears the sound of police sirens. A bunch of cops runs past her up the stairs and into her flat. They search the flat and find a trail of blood, which leads them to a cupboard.

Inside, almost unconscious, is a black man, missing three fingers and bleeding profusely. Just then, the vet arrives with the dog — fully recovered. He tells her he found three black fingers in the Rottweiler's throat, and had drawn the obvious conclusion.

If that isn't a cautionary tale, nothing is, but in the South African context, it takes on additional shades of meaning, if you'll excuse the pun. Beside the perils of young women moving to the big city, of living alone, of keeping a dog cooped up in a flat etc, there is the almost automatic acceptance that the burglar will be black.

In the US, as Brunvand points out, the consistent themes in the variations of the story point clearly to fearful current concerns about threats of burglary and violent crimes.

'The negative racial reference in oral versions of the story simply reflects the racism in our society in general.'

In South Africa, it goes further. The fact that the burglar is still inside the apartment when the woman arrives home, capable of visiting who knows what misdeeds on her, suggests serious paranoia. Since South African society is broadly characterised by a privileged white minority that exists in fear of being 'invaded' by an increasingly militant black majority, but still protected by white-dominated security structures, the legend becomes, as Ronge would say, a compelling metaphor for our times.

Much the same could be said of the various car-theft legends doing the rounds. Contrary to the old saying that a man's home is his castle, South African men often behave as if their cars are their castles. As a result, according to urban legend morality, they have to be punished, as they have allowed traditional values to succumb to mechanical luxury.

Not that these particular legends exact a heavy tax ...

The Stolen Hubcaps

This happened to my father (said the speaker). He had just bought a brand new Opel Rekord, when the two right-hand side hubcaps were stolen. He was driving in town a couple of days later when a little black guy comes up to him and says, 'Do you want to buy two hubcaps, cheap?'

So he thinks well, it would be cheaper than buying spares, and he accepts the offer. When he gets home, the two hubcaps on the other side are missing. The guy had stolen them off the car in the traffic, and had sold them back to my dad.

This is an early version, along with an apparent named victim, of a favourite Johannesburg legend. My informant told me it happened in about 1968, and he actually remembered the hubcaps initially being stolen. However, he had no direct proof of the rest of the story, and was reluctant to insist it was true, although he was 'reasonably' certain.

The 1980s version usually involves a Mercedes driver who discovers two hubcaps are missing. These are really of the expensive variety, and he is not charmed at all.

A few days later, he is speeding to Vereeniging and passes the spot on the highway near Johannesburg where a guy is doing great business selling hubcaps on the cheap. The driver does a U-turn and screeches to a halt beside the hubcap stall.

He gets out and goes to look at the wares on display. Sure enough, there are two Mercedes hubcaps for sale, cheap. And sure enough, he recognises their markings — they are his own.

In some versions, he gets home and discovers the other two hubcaps have now been stolen.

Why the muses of urban legends should be bothered about hubcaps is a mystery, but perhaps they are just part of a very much broader category of crime and car legends. A small sub-category of those legends pops up from time to time:

The Duplicate Merc Keys

Not so long ago, a chap who worked in an office block in Sandton asked his driver to take his Merc to the garage to fill up the tank. He handed him the keys, and off the driver went.

A little later, there was a huge commotion outside the building. A visitor to the offices had come out to find that his car — also a Mercedes — had been stolen. The police were called in.

When the first chap went out to see what all the noise was about, he noticed with surprise that his white Merc was still in the parking lot. Next thing, he saw his driver coming in through the main gates — driving a white Merc. It turned out that, in a million-to-one chance, the two cars, which had been parked next to each other, could be opened by the same keys.

Hearing this legend suddenly reminded me of something I was told around 1987, while riding in a bus from the city through Hillbrow. An elderly man sitting next to me suddenly pointed to a car that had drawn up alongside the bus. It was a Colt Galant.

'Did you know,' he said, 'that they only ever made seven different keys for the Galant?'

How did he know that, I asked.

'I once owned one which was stolen. When I reported it to the police, they told me it was the easiest car of all to steal: you just had to get the set of seven keys and you could get in and drive off with any Galant.'

16

STRANGER IN A STRANGE LAND

Rare is the urban legend which does not express some kind of prejudice against strangers or foreigners or their products. Even computer legends and appliance myths express fears of a stranger in our midst.

Usually, the prejudice is fairly subtle, expressed only by implication. However, where travel tales are concerned, subtlety goes out the window. This is the urban legend heartland of suspicion, hostility and prejudice. Here is the innocent abroad amid the cut-throat, savage foreigners. And here, too, is the twist in the tail, just in case things get too simple.

The point is best illustrated by an authentic South African version of a popular American legend, as told by someone who knew someone who was a friend of the employer of the victim:

The Lady in the Elevator

It happened to this little old lady who works for a Johannesburg accountant — a friend of mine told me about it (he's a friend of the accountant). She went to New York on her first overseas trip. Her boss and everyone else warned her about muggers in New York and specifically told her: 'Watch out for the black people there — they're all muggers.'

Already frightened, she booked into her hotel on the morning of her arrival and was shown to her room on the 27th floor. She unpacked, but remained in her room until late afternoon before plucking up the courage to go downstairs. Finally, she found her way to the lift. On the 20th floor a large black man got in with a big dog. The little old lady was terrified. Now she was going to get raped for sure, she thought. To make matters worse, the dog began to sniff at her dress.

Suddenly the black man said in a menacing voice, 'Down, Lady!'

Petrified, she instantly crouched down in a corner of the lift, took off her rings and held them out to him, in the hope that he would then leave her alone. Stony-faced, he ignored her and she was left unassaulted. The next day, when she went to pay the hotel bill, she found it had already been paid. By that man in the lift. Who happened to be Lionel Ritchie.

One would have thought Lionel Ritchie was hardly an intimidating sight, but perhaps little old white ladies are supposed to find any black man intimidating, certainly in urban legends.

Another South African version has Stevie Wonder doing the honours, along with his guide dog, which makes one wonder at the paranoia of elderly women who find even blind black men alarming.

The legend sends mixed signals, as the apparent racist attitude of the story is completely turned on its head in the climax. On that level, perhaps it is another of those 'healing' legends, cautioning people against making rash judgements about other people because of their skin colour. It is also, unusually, a cautionary tale against cautionary tales, telling us not to listen to every scare story we hear about foreign places.

The archetypal version of this story seems relatively new in the United States. Jan Brunvand traced it to a column by Jack Jones of the Rochester (New York state) newspaper, *Democrat and Chronicle*, of 5 January 1982:

... three unidentified Rochester women ... recently visited New York (city).

The women were in an elevator. A black man got in the elevator with a dog.

The elevator closed.

'Sit!' the man commanded.

The three women sat.

The man apologised and explained to the women that he was talking to his dog.

The women then nervously said that they were new to New York, and asked the nice man if he knew of a good restaurant.

The women went to the restaurant recommended by the man. They had a good meal, and called for their check. The waiter explained that the check had been paid by Reggie Jackson – the man they had met in the elevator.

Jack Jones actually contacted Reggie Jackson — a legendary New York baseball player then living in California. Jackson said he'd heard the story a thousand times, but it wasn't true: he wouldn't be so cruel as to keep a dog in New York City.

It then emerged that a similar story had been told in the *Cincinnati Enquirer* on 4 January 1982. Columnist Frank Weikel credited it to a businessman who said it happened to a friend of a relative — an 'impeccable source'.

Finally, it seemed that a similar event had occurred in an episode of the Bob Newhart show, involving a black man with a white dog, who gave the command, 'Sit, Whitey!' Newhart confirmed the scene, but could not remember when it had been broadcast.

Meanwhile, Jackson told a Toronto writer that the legend had started about two and a half years before. Other versions included equally famous baseball stars, and sometimes boxers.

Sports editor of the *Salt Lake Tribune*, John Mooney, whose report of the story on 29 July 1982 made it clear he thought it had really happened, concluded: 'Now doesn't that make you feel better this morning, realizing that most of the athletes are really decent folks underneath all the bickerings and scandals?'

Reggie Jackson's agent, Matt Merola, clearly saw the benefits of the story. He told the Boston *Globe*, 'I tell everyone it's true. It's a nice story, a good story, if you want it to be true, it's true!'

And the same goes for most urban legends. If you want it to be true, then let it be true!

Like this one, that really happened to an elderly woman who was a friend of a friend of the family of one of my informants:

The Purloined Biscuits

She came from a small *platteland* town — definitely a staunch Conservative Party supporter. She was travelling in America, going to visit her daughter there for the first time. After flying to New York, she was taking a train overland to get to her daughter somewhere in the Midwest.

At a railway station in a small town, the train had to stop for a while. She went into the restaurant at the station, bought a packet of biscuits, and sat down at the only table.

Next thing a black man sat down at the same table. She didn't like this, but this wasn't her country, she knew, and blacks had equal rights here. So she ignored him, and opened the packet of biscuits, which lay on the table between them.

She took a biscuit, and began eating. Next thing, he helped himself to a biscuit too, and began eating.

She was outraged, but her upbringing kept her in check — she was too well-mannered to make a scene. She just glared at him instead. She took another biscuit, and he took another one. They stared at each other.

Finally, he took the last biscuit, broke it in two, and offered her half. She was horrified — there was no way she would eat the biscuit he had touched. She got up and stormed out. As she rushed out, she happened to glance down, and saw her own packet of biscuits sticking out of her bag.

Talk about turning the tables.

The tale is structurally almost identical to The Lady in the Elevator, with similar menace, meaning and message.

Perhaps its best-known variation appears in Douglas Adams' book *So Long and Thanks for All the Fish*, the fourth and final volume in the *Hitchhiker's Guide to the Galaxy* series. A character in the book tells the story as a true one, which takes place in a railway station in England. The apparent villain, at the start, is a Pakistani, who performs his role with impeccable politeness.

Paul Smith tells another British variation in his volume, *The Book of Nastier Legends.* It takes place in a department store cafeteria in Southampton and, instead of biscuits, it's a slab of Kit Kat chocolate. Instead of the racial stereotype sitting down at her table, this one is a wild punk rocker:

> *... she picked up the Kit Kat from the table, opened it and broke it into two strips. She then broke one strip into two, put one half in her mouth and was amazed to see the punk lean over, take the other half and eat it. Not knowing quite what to do she decided to pretend that nothing had happened and proceeded to halve the remaining strip, only to have the same thing happen again.*
>
> *She finished her coffee, seething with rage, and was just about to leave when she thought, 'Right, I'll have you my lad!' Standing up, she grabbed the large doughnut*

which lay on a plate in front of the punk. She took a huge bite out of it, picked up her bags and rushed out of the cafeteria with all the speed and dignity she could muster.

On the way home she related this incident and bemoaned the ignorance of today's youth to the woman sitting next to her on the bus. Suddenly, searching for her purse to pay her bus fare, she found in her bag the Kit Kat she had bought in the cafeteria.

In *The Choking Doberman*, Jan Brunvand refers to the story as an English legend which was reported as long ago as 1972 by British folklorist AW Smith. The location in each of three stories always involved rail travel, and people of different race groups to the culprit (a Pakistani, a West Indian and an African).

Smith pointed to 'the patient and indeed saintly character of the often despised and rejected'.

However, he felt the tale to be of American origin, due to various American usages in some versions.

An Irish version was reported to have happened at the station in Belfast, where the traveller says to the black man, 'Excuse me, but we don't do that in this country.' This echoes almost precisely the words of Douglas Adams' traveller.

More recently, an indigenous American version has surfaced, involving a traveller, a packet (or two) of Oreo cookies and a young man of unspecified race.

A New Zealand version, published in the *Pegasus Post* of Christchurch on 29 April 1985, involves an 80-year-old woman, a punk rocker and a Moro chocolate bar. Clearly a descendant of the Kit Kat version.

The upshot, generally, is a strong message to older people to set aside their prejudices about people of other races as well as of the youth. Persist in your suspicion, it warns, and your hostility will be punished. Not only that, but you will find that *you* are guilty of the things you attribute to strangers.

As I said, urban legends are not exactly subtle.

The next story is a South African variation of an extremely tasteless and extremely funny American legend, as told by Gus Silber in *Style*:

The Vanishing Grandmother

One week before Christmas, a farming family from Venterspost drove to Durban to see the sea. Actually, only the father drove — the mother sat in front, and the four kids and the grandmother squashed shoulders in the back. It was a Studebaker. The luggage was on the roof-rack. The grandmother was ninety-seven. Shame: everyone knew she would never see Durban again.

Halfway between Kroonstad and Harrismith, she died in her sleep, although it was not until Vryheid, when the Studebaker stopped for sandwiches, that anyone noticed. The road was deserted and help was a long hot drive away. Help for the kids, not the grandmother. Their anguish was infectious: it wasn't so much that they missed their grandmother, it was because the grandmother was still there.

There was only one practical thing to do. The father wrapped the grandmother in a groundsheet and swapped her for the luggage. Everyone climbed out at the police station. Except the grandmother.

There was much to explain and many forms to fill in. It was some time later that the father patted his pocket with concern. The keys were not there. He rushed outside. The Studebaker had been stolen. It has not been seen to this day, and grandmother will never see Durban again.

The best-known version of this legend occurs in the film *National Lampoon's Vacation*, starring Chevy Chase.

Granny dies in stationwagon taking family to Wallyworld (parody of Walt Disney World). She is due to be dropped off at relatives en route, but dies first. Kids refuse to ride with corpse, daddy wraps her in blanket, ties her on roof-rack. At drop-off point, relatives are out. Daddy sets granny down on lawn chair, with note attached.

One local film critic howled his outrage at the film, describing the scene as being in extremely bad taste. I do not suggest he travel in urban legend country.

Jan Brunvand found the first text of the Runaway Grandmother, as he called the tale, in a folklore study published in 1963, as told by an Englishwoman who heard it in Canada from a cousin who had first heard it in Leeds, England. Even then, therefore, it was an old story.

The earliest published American version appeared as a news article in the San José *Mercury*, also in 1963. Folklorist Robert H Woodward paraphrased it like this:

> *A local resident reports as fact an experience of a Washington State family that he knows. After the family had crossed the Mexican border on a vacation trip, one of the children said, 'Mama, Grandma won't wake up.' Upon discovering that Grandma had died, the family placed her body in a sleeping bag and secured her to the top of their automobile, planning to report her death to the police at the first town. While they were in the station, their car was stolen – with Grandma's body still aboard. No trace has yet been found of either Grandma or the car. Another resident reports the tale as having happened in Italy.*

It just goes to show how well travelled urban legends can be. English folklorist Stewart Sanderson reported that he had first heard the story in Leeds in 1960, 'from the wife of a colleague who told it as having happened to friends of her friends in Brussels, as they escaped through northern

185

France during the German invasion of 1940'.

He collected a subsequent version at the University of Nsukka, Nigeria, in 1965.

In this version, which brings us much closer to home, 'the body of an old woman, being taken back for burial at her native village on the Crow river, is lost by rolling off the roof of a mammy-wagon (the local bus) into the bush.'

Indiana folklorist Linda Degh suggests that the message of the story derives from 'the fear of the return of the dead' and expresses the common concern that 'the corpse has to receive a decent burial'.

Another folklorist, Alan Dundes, suggested that the basic message was the rejection of old age and dying in our 'youth-oriented society'.

17 HAVE I GOT A VIRUS FOR YOU!

Right now, as I sit at my computer to type in this chapter, I have a timely newspaper report before me. Today is Friday, 13 July 1990. This afternoon edition of the *Star* carries the following story on its foreign page:

> *As another Friday the 13th dawns, computer-users around the world wait nervously to see whether the industry's most notorious disk 'virus' will strike again. The Friday 13th computer virus, believed to have originated in Israel, is now believed to lurk in hundreds of thousands of systems around the world, ready to be activated every time the critical date comes around.*

It is now evening and, while I did see a black cat behaving suspiciously under a ladder earlier, I am not aware of the collapse of Civilisation As We Know It.

However, I did not expect the destruction of global economies or even individual data-bases today. This is the fourth time in three months that the world — or South Africa — has faced electronic chaos.

On Wednesday, 18 April 1990, the morning newspaper *Beeld* informed us that we had escaped two awful computer viruses over the Easter weekend that had just ended:

'The two viruses were intended to strike last Friday and Saturday, but by yesterday no panic calls had been received from anyone whose computer had been affected by the viruses, said Mr Martin Olivier of the CSIR (Council for Scientific and Industrial Research) computer virus division.'

Beeld identified the viruses as 'the well-known' Jerusalem virus, which is activated on any Friday the 13th', and 'the new Durban virus, that wreaks its havoc when the 14th of the month falls on a Saturday'.

According to *Beeld*, the Jerusalem virus first appeared on Friday, 13 October 1989, causing 'virus-fever' among the owners of personal computers.

Olivier suggested the lack of panic on 13 April 1990 was due to the day being a public holiday when most people would not be using their computers. The same applied to the Durban virus. In addition, the latter had not spread far enough, or had been wiped out completely. He was only aware of one company where it had previously emerged, and it was quickly dealt with.

Despite this damp squib, the article concluded by warning that the next Friday 13th and Saturday 14th was due in July. Well, here we are and my computer has yet to å§%?£$*&.

Seriously, though, these warnings have become tedious to many computer users, who almost hope something *will* happen so that they can see what all the fuss is about. The next alert date was 16 June, the anniversary of the 1976 Soweto uprising (urban legends love anniversaries).

On 22 May 1990, the *Star* had reported the first 'political' computer virus.

Ian Melamed, managing director of Business Systems Solutions, told the *Star* it was called the 'Pretoria virus', or 'June 16th virus', and it 'was definitely written with a political influence. It is designed to go off on Soweto Day.'

The date 16 June 1976 changed the face of South African politics forever, and still has connotations of violence and revolution for most white South Africans, while it represents a time of mourning and of hope for liberation for blacks.

To Melamed, it clearly spelt anarchy, at least in the computer industry. He added that 'the possible suspect is known to members of the industry and action will be taken

188

against the culprit once enough evidence is available'.

Unfortunately, urban legends do not leave 'enough evidence'. They do, however, regularly leave 'possible' suspects, but the legal world would have a serious problem with that phrasing.

To date, I am aware of no 16 June computer collapse, no evidence reported, and no action announced against any culprit. If someone did devise a virus to go off on 16 June, it didn't work, again confining the story to the realm of legend.

Are any of these apocalyptic computer viruses genuine, or are they simply urban legends born out of the paranoia of computer users? After all, anyone working on a stand-alone computer knows the irritation of trying to get it to behave according to the sales pitch on the package. And anyone who uses a computer network knows the frustration of systems developing gremlins or constantly 'crashing'.

First, the facts: Computer viruses do exist. Some are created as a prank, others through pure malice. They spread like any respectable sexual disease would, by your playing with software that isn't yours.

Prime breeding grounds are university computer faculties, where every student seems to be trying to out-innovate the next, or is engaged in a flourishing exchange market for nifty new pirated software.

The analogy has often been made to Aids: the spread of a virus is geometric. One infected system spreads the virus to ten others, which spread it to a hundred, then a thousand, and so on.

Let us take a brief look at some of the most famous viruses:

* The Cookie Monster. It flashes the message WANT COOKIE on your screen. If you do not immediately type in COOKIE, it proceeds to destroy your database. This is possibly the grandaddy of them all, and was itself reported

as an urban legend when it first emerged.

* The Disk Killer. According to *Sunday Star* computer columnist Jennigay Coetzer, it is activated once a machine has been in use for 48 hours non-stop. It proceeds to format your hard drive, ie clean it out totally, but not before flashing up the message: DISK KILLER BY COMPUTER OGRE. According to Martin Olivier, it first appeared in South Africa in February 1990.

* The Stoned Virus. It garbles whatever you have typed on screen, freezes all operations, then announces THIS COMPUTER IS STONED. A cousin of mine, whose children commute between home and their university computer bureau, counted this as the worst among forty-two apparent viruses that had infected her hard drive.

* The Sunday Virus. First reported in *Beeld* on 27 March 1990, it acts at any time, but was supposed to have been meant to be activated on Sundays. It results in regular appearances on your screen of the message: TODAY IS SUNDAY! WHY DO YOU WORK SO HARD? ALL WORK AND NO PLAY MAKES YOU A DULL BOY! COME ON! LET'S GO OUT AND HAVE SOME FUN!

I can relate to this virus. However, some versions are themselves bugged, says Coetzer. They don't display the message, but casually proceed to infect every COM and EXE file on the disk or hard drive, increasing their file size by precisely 1 636 bytes.

* Screen Crumble, or Cascade. What it sounds like it does to newly-input data, it *does* do to newly-input data.

* The Brain Virus. Mostly found in schools. Not regarded as terminal.

* The 4096 Virus. Like the Sunday virus, it disarms any 'memory-resident protection', and then increases files by exactly 4 096 bytes. It displays the message FRODO LIVES. Tolkien would have been amused. This one is set to go off between 22 September and 31 December, for that added feeling of holiday season security. It is especially

190

toxic, says Olivier, as it does not allow the directory to show the files' new sizes, but keeps the displayed size at the original figure so that you do not know your system is infected until it crashes.

* The Bouncing Ball. What one might call a fun virus, it is really just a nuisance, and gives the user a good scare, but does little more than hop about the screen. Some versions destroy everything in the path of their bounces.

* Durban * Jerusalem and * Soweto make up the ten friendly neighbourhood viruses, but it is the last three that concern us most here.

Firstly, let us look at a little more context. According to Ian Melamed, as reported in the *Sunday Star* of 27 May 1990, his courses on handling virus problems show that six out of fourteen people with computers have had experience with at least one virus. 'This compares with the United States at two out of 14, and three out of 14 in Britain.'

Melamed discussed these statistics with a German and a British virus expert, both of whom expressed surprise that the incidence here was 'so out of step with the rest of the world'. Melamed concluded that, being a smaller, closer knit community, there is a tendency to share disks in South Africa. If half the computer users in the country, therefore, have been exposed to the virus, why shouldn't they accept the existence of a slightly different virus, which just happens to be more sophisticated in that it responds to a date on the computer's internal clock?

It makes perfect sense. But it just doesn't happen. Every time a date-sensitive virus is due to strike, technical helplines and computer information services around the world go on red alert to deal with the expected flood of calls from panicked computer users. And each time they express surprise at how few calls they receive. In any event many of these calls relate to the everyday viruses.

Sure, some of these 'date' viruses are reported, and I am not saying they don't exist, but the threat of them bringing an end to the computer world appears as unlikely as any urban legend. They seem to be the stuff of paranoia and conspiracy theories, and, in any case, they are small fry compared to the real big daddy of viruses, as reported in the local *People* magazine on 5 July 1989:

COMPUTERS ARE TRYING TO CONTROL THE WORLD

A villainous virus has infected the world's network of supercomputers and could prove much more deadly than actual germ warfare in destroying mankind.

Experts have discovered that killer computers have developed a sinister internal plot which will cause malfunctions, destroy data, and disrupt important everyday operations.

The result will be panic and havoc everywhere.

Computer foul-ups could send millions to their deaths by triggering nuclear attacks, or sabotaging airline traffic control systems.

So-called computer viruses have always been blamed on hackers with a bad sense of humour.

But investigators have discovered the computers themselves have been causing some of the troubles.

Japanese computer whiz Nikko Surishima stumbled onto the amazing find during a routine overhaul.

'I first thought the virus was created by a data processor having sadistic fun, but I soon found out it's the doings of smart computers,' said Nikko, who died in a suspicious fashion shortly after the discovery. The 34-year-old technician was electrocuted while trying to de-programme a super-computer. His log books leave evidence of a major plot.

'One day I heard a machine equipped with a voice synthesizer utter "Our masters will be destroyed." It gave me goosebumps,' writes Nikko.

'On another occasion, a display screen flashed the message, "The world belongs to us." The words were gone in an instant. It was like the computer was taunting me.

'I realise now mankind must take drastic measures quickly to stop these machines bent on world control.'

Now that is what I call a computer virus. No messing around with Cookie Monsters and Bouncing Balls here. We're talking big league.

Unfortunately, it has been done before, most notably by HAL, the computer in Stanley Kubrick's *2001: A Space Odyssey*, and also in hundreds of weak science fiction stories and low-budget Japanese films. It is such a cliché, it ... might just be true?

While this story may read like an urban legend, particularly with that ominous warning at the end, it has a few problem areas. For instance, who would believe a data-processor having fun?

Actually, the story falls short due to the lack of any kind of official comment, however fictional, of the kind that is usually employed to give urban legends credibility. And the only 'expert' quoted is dead. But keep watching that one. It sounds like something out of 1950s American McCarthyite paranoia, as do so many urban legends.

And watch out for the ones that tell you the international financial community's computers will come crashing down simultaneously on 1 January 2000, as they're not equipped to deal with a new millennium in their internal clocks. Or that the computers of the world will freeze on the stroke of the 9th day of the 9th month of 1999.

All this implies, of course, that the viruses have to destroy the world time-zone by time-zone, since 09/09/99, or 2000 or 2001, will take 24 hours to dawn across the world.

Back in the real world, however, we may rest assured that each of these dates will spawn a fresh epidemic of warnings.

Before we get complacent about it, though, consider this: Jan Brunvand recorded the alleged workings of the Cookie Monster in 1984 in *The Choking Doberman*. The term for virus in those days was 'mystery glitch'. Brunvand made a strong case for it being an urban legend, based largely on the technical advice of a computer expert who explained to him in great detail why these 'glitches' probably could not be introduced into a computer. Brunvand did point out, however, that the *Wall Street Journal* had treated the Cookie Monster as a true story in its issue of 13 April 1983.

At the time, it was easy to ascribe it to part of an emergent folklore about computers. In fact, most of the early scare stories were just legends. Today they are reality, with technical ability having caught up with paranoid fantasy. Ten years from now, super-viruses may well have been spawned to bring new meaning to the phrase Red Letter Day.

Technology proceeds apace, and folklore follows in its wake, or leads it. As new forms of technology emerge, new misunderstandings arise and, as a result, new urban legends begin to circulate.

Not only are people generally reticent about new technology, they are downright suspicious of it and, in some cases, paranoid. It is known as technophobia.

Computer viruses serve the technophobic well. What was just an emergent folklore in the early 1980s is now an area rife with urban legend, myth and fallacy — complete with firm 'believers' who are ready to throw a punch at anyone who dares to dispute their given wisdom.

18   TEENAGE MUTANT LEGENDS

Yank at a neurosis and a legend will come tumbling out. Many urban legends express the 'danger within' — the evil menace that lurks unseen in our homes or neighbourhoods. In most cases, the menace is of a cold, calculating, murderous variety. And it is usually human.

But then there are animal legends. And we're not talking Aesop's Fables. We're talking vicious mutant alligators, tragically exploding puppies, and mutant ninja fleas.

The Resettled Reptile

The archetypal animal urban legend is about as urban as they get: the supposed mutant alligators in the New York sewers.

As legend has it, families that used to take vacations to Florida's Everglades swamps would come back with one of those cute, tiny baby alligators to keep as pets in their New York apartments. By and by the alligator would grow large enough to compete with the household fox terrier for its dogfood, and they would regretfully flush it (the alligator, not the dog) down the toilet. The resettled reptile would soon find itself in the sewers of the metropolis, with nothing to live on but human waste, toxic substances and radioactive matter. This of course mutates the alligator, which grows into a huge monster. As a result of its environment, it is also often snow white and blind.

While this is obviously not a South African legend, it is often told here, and has developed local variants. There is an element of truth in the original legend.

On 10 February 1935 the *New York Times* reported that a group of teenagers had dragged a live eight-foot alligator out of a sewer in Harlem the previous evening. They had been shovelling snow into a manhole, they claimed, when they saw the creature thrashing about in the sewer ten feet below them. They decided to drag it out with a clothesline, and get it onto dry land, whereupon the creature, as is an alligator's wont, began snapping at them. They reacted by beating it to death.

Cecil Adams, the apparently mythical American newspaper columnist who supposedly pens the column 'The Straight Dope' in the *Chicago Reader*, wrote in 'The Straight Dope' compilation volume: 'It's questionable whether the alligators could actually be said to have "lived" in the ... sewers.

'The locals at the time speculated that the animal had fallen from a boat passing through the nearby Harlem River and had swum 150 yards up a storm conduit.'

Adams, who claims to have the correct answer to any question, does, however, give the opposition its say. He quotes from a 1959 book by Robert Daley called *The World Beneath the City*. In this account of New York's underground utilities, a former sewer superintendent named Teddy May claimed to have seen alligators with his own eyes during an inspection tour around 1935. He had heard stories about the alligators from sewer workers, but had thought they were only kidding before he finally saw them himself.

However, these alligators were a mere two feet long, and papers apparently speculated that the parents had bought them for their children during a passing fad, had grown tired of them, and flushed them away.

Teddy May had a more permanent solution. He sent sewer workers in with poison and even firearms. The alligators were wiped out, and the urban legend was born.

And so we come to 1990, and the release of the box-office smash *Teenage Mutant Ninja Turtles*. It is the story of four turtles who are dropped into the sewers beneath New York, and accidentally get splashed with a 'mutagen'. They naturally mutate into large, human-like turtles, with a curious command of the American language and a taste for pizza. They meet a ninja master who has mutated into a rat, and he takes them under his wing.

On 8 April 1990, on cue, the following report appeared in the *Sunday Times*:

MUTANT TURTLE MOVIE IS TRUE

Monster turtles have been found in the sewers of New York – as a horror film about shellbacked mutants sweeps America.

The not-so-jolly green giants, which bite wildly at anything in their path, weigh in at 22 kg each – ten times the normal size.

Conservationist John Reidy said radioactive waste might have made them grow like the creatures in the hit film Teenage Mutant Ninja Turtles, *which grossed R64-million in its first two days.*

Publicity stunt? Or urban legend?

A month later came a wire-service report from Venice, Italy, that mutant fleas were attacking locals and tourists, inflicting bites that turned into rashes, blisters and allergic boils. This time it was the *Star* that took the bait. They even quoted the obligatory expert: 'We have no idea what the insect is,' said Dr Feanco D'Andrea, 'but it is thriving and reproducing on the lagoon, which has green algae patches.' The *Star* had no problem identifying the insects: they were 'teenage mutant ninja fleas'.

While this report may well be true, the turtle tale is so directly derivative of the alligator legend, it is almost

197

certainly an urban legend, with an obscure 'expert' giving the kind of absurd explanation that belongs in folklore.

It demonstrates again how a major media event can have a direct effect on modern myths. The film has turned turtles into the dominant reptilian symbol of the moment, and they have inevitably invaded other animal legends.

But then again, what if it's true? In fact, there is apparently an element of truth to the story. This time, however, it is a genuine, indigenous South African story:

The Mutant Turtles in the Dam

Years ago, there was a fad on the Witwatersrand for keeping those little green American turtles as pets. Actually, they were terrapins, and they were known as jewelnecks, because of the distinctive markings round their necks. Then the Government banned anyone keeping turtles or tortoises privately. Some people let them go in the wild, but others flushed them down their toilets.

These turtles eventually found their way, via the sewers, into suburban rivers and dams, where they lived off waste products and sewage, as well as toxic waste. This helped them grow into giant turtles, and in some dams they killed off all the fish.

Peter Esterhuysen, an oral literature specialist, says that the story was told throughout the Witwatersrand during the 1970s, and he believes it was a typical urban legend of the time. However, he had first-hand experience to back it up:

While I was growing up in Florida (on the East Rand) we had a fishpond in our garden. Gradually the fish began to disappear, and we suspected predatory birds. We strung a net across the pond, but it didn't help. Eventually, we discovered a huge turtle in the pond — with those distinctive jewelneck markings.

The next legend was recounted by a resident of Boksburg, the town briefly infamous for attempting to reverse racial reforms in 1989. Black and 'Coloured' consumer boycotts forced the business community to force the town council to rescind their 'new' petty apartheid regulations. A central symbol of the entire controversy was Boksburg Lake, which some whites felt should be for white use only. The legend came earlier, but seems to provide an appropriate metaphor:

The Piranha in the Lake

A couple of years ago there was a big scare in the local papers. Apparently some private collector had these fish that were a relative of the Amazonian piranha.

For some reason he couldn't keep them anymore, and he dumped them in Boksburg Lake. Next thing, people began finding ducks — or rather, the skeletons of ducks — picked clean to the bone, floating on the water.

This went on for a long time, and people believed it for years.

Vaguely related to this story is the legend of ...

The Dynamite Retriever

This tale, clearly set before Namibia's independence process began in 1989, was introduced with the words, 'This is a story that a friend of mine told me that I never thought of as an urban legend until now.'

My friend went to visit a friend of his who lived on a farm in

Namibia. This friend told him that he'd introduced fish into one of his dams, and they reproduced so rapidly that they began to clog up the weirs and the filtration system. So he was having a drink one Friday evening with one of the army guys who was on duty guarding farms in the area and he told him his problem. The army guy says, 'I'll solve your problem. I'll blow them up with dynamite. I'll blow the fish out of the water ...'

So that Sunday morning he comes around and says, 'Look, you're the farmer. You have the stick (of dynamite). You can throw it in.' So he threw it in, and his devoted labrador, who was with him at the time, leaped in to retrieve it, and he started swimming back towards them. These guys ran like hell, with the dog after them, dynamite in its mouth, and the dog exploded halfway across the dam.

See? You shouldn't mess with fish.

This seems to be a cautionary tale about interfering with nature's ways. It is directly related to a popular old legend that has made its way into novels, films and folklore:

The Aardvark's Revenge

This bunch of tourists was on safari when their Landrover ran over an aardvark. They stopped and walked back to see what had happened. They found the poor creature dragging itself gamely to the side of the road.

As it was already dying, they decided to have some fun. They fetched a stick of dynamite from the Landrover and tied it to the aardvark, who was wandering into the veld to die.

They ran behind a rock to watch — and saw the bewildered animal struggle back onto the road, and go towards the Landrover. There was nothing they could do. It crawled under the vehicle and lay down to expire. It took the Landrover with it.

In this case, not only is tampering with nature severely punished, but so is cruelty to animals, disrespect for the dying, and carrying explosives on safari (I never did have that bit explained to me).

Now let's get back to fish of a different colour:

Mutant Ninja Barbels

Ever heard of the Mutant Catfish of Hartbeespoortdam? The story goes like this:

Several years ago, when the provincial authorities were clearing duckweed from Hartbeespoortdam, they made sonar scans of the bottom. They discovered that there were large moving objects — at least 30 metres long — at the bottom of the dam. Eventually they discovered they were giant catfish — barbel — living in the dam.

While this may sound like a common Loch Ness Monster type legend, it contains the urban legend element of 'validation' — authorities are said to have made the discovery, and it can be placed at a time of a specific cleanup operation, which 'proves' the story.

There even appear to be elements of traditional folklore. By coincidence, a German film released on the art-cinema circuit in South Africa in 1990, *Summer of White Roses*, tells of a community on the side of a river which is ruled by a 'river god'. The god is said to be a barbel. An entire mythology is built around the barbel in the film, suggesting there is a European catfish mythology which was transported to South Africa many years ago.

In urban legends, however, animals rarely have the power that traditional legends allow them. I have before me newspaper clippings reporting lovestruck rams killing farmers in Crete, crocodiles eating golfers in Australia, and dogs in Sweden accidentally triggering their owners' hunting rifles and killing them.

I have reports of police gaoling a rabbit in Finland (for vagrancy and loitering — 'we're just doing our duty,' police said); of laboratory rats being arrested in Tokyo after escaping from their cages on a Jumbo jet; of a woman in Kenya demanding that police gaol her dog for biting a neighbour (police refused).

How many of these will turn out to be urban legends I cannot guess, but those Kenyans bear watching. One report has a magistrate threatening to gaol two donkeys for trespassing in the courthouse.

One story that is almost certainly an urban legend appeared in the *Weekend Argus* on 7 April 1990, and told of an eagle snatching a two-year-old child near Esfahan in Iran.

The story was spotted by one WP Stanford of Somerset West, who painstakingly reviewed the related literature. He advised the *Argus* that 'the records of some 250 years, the stories and even pictures (drawn) of children being taken, have never been proved. If this incident can be proved it will make history.'

And thus it is with urban legends.

Folklorists still await photographic or substantial eyewitness evidence of a dog exploding in a microwave oven. Not that folklorists are especially ghoulish (though I wouldn't vouch for all of them), but this is probably the most widely believed of all urban legends about animals.

The Poodle in the Microwave

I first encountered this legend several years ago in Miami in the United States. It was specifically identified as an urban

202

legend which people tend to believe, and I found such gullibility amusing.

However, when I repeated it to a friend of a friend (*he* was my friend, *she* was my friend's friend) as 'one of those crazy things people believe', she was outraged at my insensitivity. It really had happened, about six months earlier, she announced. How did she know? She read it in a newspaper, she said triumphantly. Well, actually, she said, not she herself, but a friend had read it, and told her about it. She would call the friend the next day and find out exactly when it had happened.

She never did, and is no longer a friend of my friend (due to unrelated complications), but I have some small consolation for her: microwaved pet reports *do* appear in newspapers.

Most recently in South Africa, the *Star* reported a 'semi-microwaved schnauzer' on 30 September 1989, while the *Sunday Times* reported a 'defrosted dog' on 14 January 1990. Both survived, suggesting that urban legends have become kinder and gentler with the dawning of the 1990s.

The schnauzer provides folklorists with unusually specific detail:

POOCH WAS MICROWAVED

TORONTO – Kizi, the miniature schnauzer dog, is recovering after an intruder popped her in the oven. Kizi escaped with a limp and a burnt ear after her ordeal, her owner said.

'We think he set the timer for nine minutes. She had a metal buckle on her collar and that shorted the oven. That saved her life,' said Kizi's owner, 13-year-old Chad Leis of Kitchener, Ontario. A 14-year-old boy has been charged with cruelty.

The microwaved pet is more usually a poodle, and the story usually goes like this:

An old lady was given a microwave by her children. One day, not quite *au fait* with its applications, after bathing her dog she put it in the microwave to dry it off. Suddenly there was a loud bang. The unfortunate dog had exploded.

Some versions have a small boy, still innocent about the dangers of microwaves, doing the damage. Others have the animal cooking from inside out, which more appropriately describes the effect of microwaves on food.

Although the legend ties in directly to suspicion of new technology, it appears that the microwave oven is not essential to the legend: it was current in the 1960s in tales about pets crawling into gas ovens or tumble dryers and meeting their destiny.

The grandaddy of the microwave version, however, apparently first appeared in the film *Getting Wasted,* a 1970 parody of the Elliot Gould hit *Getting Straight*. In the movie, the family poodle goes to its maker via a tasteless scene in the family's brand new microwave oven. The ovens had, incidentally, just come on the market.

And now, the South African version, in all its local-nuance glory, as recounted by Gus Silber in *Style*:

> *On her way to the beauty parlour, the madam noticed, to her dismay, that Tutu the French poodle was unclean. She stopped. 'Beauty!'*
>
> *Beauty shuffled into the hallway, wiped her sudsy hands on her apron that said WORLD'S GREATEST MAID. This had been her Christmas present from the madam. (Tutu had got a gift-wrapped diamond choker.) 'Listen, Beauty,' said the madam, her eyes disguised by chrome, 'I want you to give Tutu a nice clean bath for me, okay?'*
>
> *The madam rubbed her fist against her palm to indicate the action required, and continued: 'You dry my baby nicely, see? I don't want him to catch cold.'*

When she had finished the pots and the pans and the wok and the goblets, and when she had made the beds and scrubbed the floors and Hoovered the carpets, and when she had Jikked the toilets and Vimmed the bathrooms and Zebbed the kitchen, and when she had coaxed the dog from under the madam's bed with a Romany Cream, Beauty, whose real name was Nomavenda, washed Tutu nicely. Grey as a dishrag, growling, shivering under his perm, Tutu leaped from his bathtub and rolled deliriously in the dirt.

This happened twice. The madam was due back soon. She would shout. Beauty grabbed Tutu like a wrestler, soaped and sponged and rinsed him, wrapped him in a towel, and put him in the microwave oven to dry. Tutu did not catch cold. He dried in seconds, and cooked from the inside. Before Beauty hit the floor, she noticed something else. If you put a whole potato in a microwave oven and leave it for a while, it pops.

Talk about divine retribution. The original legend is mere technophobia. This one is culture-clash, hubris punished, technological menace and worker exploitation all rolled into one.

While it is clearly not a 'folk narrative' — a version recounted as true in normal conversation — it is an effective amalgamation of several sources of underlying tension in suburban life. The madam who thinks of herself as The Madam; whose life revolves around the beauty parlour; her disrespect for black leaders as revealed in naming the dog after the Nobel Peace Prize winner; her ignorance of black culture reflected in her using a bland clichéd 'Christian' name like Beauty when the employee's true, given name is so much more evocative; her manner of treating her dog with more respect than the maid; the imperious nature of the madam-maid relationship; the sheer exploitation.

All these are real, and common in white suburbia. All slot

comfortably into suburban varieties of urban legends. It is indeed a cautionary tale for our times.

19 URBAN LEGENDS: THE NEXT GENERATION

Most 'new' urban legends, it seems, turn out to be old legends, appropriately updated. Many legends are merely derivatives or variations of older legends. Some can be traced back to medieval times, to the ancient Roman and Greek civilisations, even to biblical times.

But of course, new urban legends *are* born all the time. It may not be possible to invent an urban legend — that is, to make one up and engineer events in such a way that it becomes accepted as an urban legend supposedly passed down through oral culture — but there is a difference between creating an urban legend and discovering that one has been created. In fact, urban legends aren't really created: they emerge, from somewhere in the depths of popular consciousness and culture.

It may not be easy to make up an urban legend, but it is not difficult for an urban legend to start up.

We can expect new tales to crop up in areas that are major preoccupations of the human psyche, but also in those areas which seem so trivial, one would hardly expect them to occupy room in any individual mind, let alone the mass consciousness.

While urban legends do not respect geographical borders, the South African experience is obviously fertile soil for new legends. Fear and hope for the future, racial prejudice and the like, will almost certainly be behind much of the emergent folklore.

The process will serve all sections of the political spectrum, illustrating stupidity, arrogance, ignorance, viciousness — whatever you want — of any and all the racial or political groups.

The progression from a repressed society to a politically liberated society is also likely to reveal itself in sexual politics — not in terms of promiscuity, but with regard to awareness, knowledge and openness about the issue. The issue will prey on many a subconscious, not to mention conscious mind, and the area is ripe for new legends.

We have already seen the emergence of a large body of myth and folklore surrounding the Aids issue, and this should have come as no surprise. After all, what can be more fearful than a killer disease that is caused by the pursuit of physical pleasure, that can lie dormant for years, that you can pick up anywhere, that turns sex into a game of Russian Roulette.

We can expect to see many more Aids legends. Those we have seen perfectly illustrate the diverse nature of urban legends, in that there are tales ranging from the trivial, personal and sometimes amusing, all the way through to the full-blown global conspiracy theory.

Terminal diseases are a major preoccupation of our time, and are entering folklore via the strangest routes. A recent ongoing news story already seems to be taking on elements of legend, even as the factual basis of the legend is still being aired in the media.

It all began when a terminally ill child by the name of Mario Morby entered the *Guinness Book of Records* in 1987 for the most get-well cards ever received by one person — a total of 1 000 265. According to Donald McFarlane, editor of the *Book of Records*, the child, now 13, is recovering from his leukemia yet his family is still receiving cards three years later.

Last year, 10-year-old Craig Shergold, who suffers from a rare form of brain cancer, decided to challenge the record. McFarlane tried to dissuade his family, and warned them that the bid could spiral out of control.

In an Associated Press report published by the *Star* on 30 June 1990, McFarlane told journalist Jessica Baldwin, 'Our experience is that once it goes international, it is absolutely unstoppable.'

Baldwin reports that the get-well card category was discontinued after the Morby record, but McFarlane revived it after intense pressure. It is that pressure that makes the story's entrance into legend inevitable.

When the Shergold appeal went round the world, it eventually reached South Africa. It was disseminated largely via fax machines (do I detect an emergent fax folklore?). People who received the faxes were often so moved, they made copies for their entire offices, or themselves sent it out as a fax to all their contacts.

Along with some colleagues, I felt the appeal to be in rather bad taste, not because of the child's motives, but because of the emotional blackmail that it inspired in other colleagues. They took our refusal to send cards as a reflection of callousness and heartless cynicism, and told us so in no uncertain terms.

That is when I realised we were dealing with an urban legend in the making. Refutation of urban legends inspires exactly this kind of self-righteous, hostile, emotional abuse from people who are otherwise quite amiable and rational.

Jessica Baldwin's report was sweet vindication for those of us who held out against the onslaught (not to mention for Donald McFarlane):

> *Craig ... broke the record months ago, but the cards keep coming. More than 16-million have arrived.*
>
> *'We don't want any more cards because it looks as though we're taking cards for no reason,' Craig's mother, Marion, said from the family home in Carshalton, near London. 'Every card says "we hope you make it in the record books", so it seems kind of greedy to keep accepting them,' she said.*

> ... *(McFarlane said) 'I thought I had decided over a year ago that (Mario Morby) would be the last one, but it is very difficult to hold out against an emotive press. I couldn't do my job – well-intentioned, very sentimental people called me at work and I received quite a lot of hate mail, including one that said: "If you have children I hope they die of cancer." '*
>
> ... *The editor said he was trying to protect the Shergolds 'from an ugly situation, particularly if Craig had died. The cards would have kept coming.'*
>
> *Craig had an operation in January 1988 that removed three-quarters of a brain tumour. Marion Shergold said doctors believe chemotherapy and radiotherapy have successfully stemmed the disease's spread into his spinal cord.*

Would the two recoveries kill the legend? Not likely. Several years ago, Gwen Gill, the *Sunday Times'* 'Columnist Who Cares', received a similar appeal, possibly Mario Morby's. She thought no more of it, she says, until she received another appeal earlier this year, for a Scottish child. She published it, but with reservations.

A week later, her doubts were confirmed when a local reader of Scottish origin sent her a clipping from a newspaper published in his former hometown — and the home of this latest terminally ill patient. It quoted the local postmaster complaining that his office had been flooded with get-well cards — sent to an address that didn't exist, and to a person who didn't exist either.

However, had anyone refused a request from the office's resident sentimentalist to send a card to this address, well-intentioned dismay and anger would have shamed the person into relenting.

Even if every case were proved to be a myth, it is the kind of story that does not succumb to rational discussion.

Urban legend as emotional blackmail? You'd better

believe it.

Another area ready for the legend treatment is the apparent transformation from the 1980s 'Greed decade' into the 1990s 'Green decade'. Magazine articles trumpet the death of the Yuppie, George Bush waffles about a 'kinder, gentler America', and generally the money-madness of the 1980s — a Power Decade, if ever there was one — is being buried under the righteousness and self-righteousness of the 1990s.

This suggests new legends that reflect the come-uppance of the truly rich and powerful. Expect a few Donald Trump legends. Who does not better represent the egotistical greed of the 1980s, the determination to show off wealth as never before? Yachts, casinos, hotels, sports events carried his name. There must be an urban legend lurking somewhere there.

Disgraced junk bond wizards Ivan Boesky and Mike Milken are equally ripe for legend. One can well imagine TV programmes like 'Lifestyles of the Rich and Famous' giving way to 'What Happened to the Rich and Famous?'

In South Africa, someone like Sun City originator Sol Kerzner may also be due for this kind of treatment. In a strange parallel to the American experience, Kerzner effectively lost his power to run the gambling empires of the Transkei, and that homeland attempted to have him extradited from South Africa on bribery charges. His nickname, the Sun King, begs a legend or two.

There is a direct link between corporate greed and environmental despoliation. We can expect to see 'new' legends concerning ecology, and certainly regarding contamination of our foodstuffs. These legends have been around for decades, but we can surely expect to see them taking a firmer grip on the land of urban legends.

These will sometimes be related to conspiracy theories, but will probably deal more often with the dangers of the modern environment, rather than corporate culpability.

These stories — as with many other new legends we can expect — will often be rooted in factual events. Usually, however, their roots will be as elusive as any urban legend. And sometimes, just sometimes, an urban legend may even be true!

Acknowledgements

Every legend in this book has a story behind it — but then so does the book itself. It is the story of dozens of people who have unselfishly passed on their stories and legends, rumours and myths, and given me their time and support — for a project which has been close to my heart for five years.

There are three people to whom I am especially indebted.

The first is Sheryl Lack, whose unswerving commitment to the book made it almost as much her project as mine. Secondly, Gus Silber, a fellow-traveller in the land of urban legends, who always seems to have popped up at crucial moments in my career. And thirdly, Jan Harold Brunvand, the man who is to urban legends what salt is to popcorn, who first inspired my interest without knowing it, and then directly encouraged it.

Several other people have made valuable contributions: Alison Lowry of Penguin, who recognised the worthiness of the project from the start; Peter Esterhuysen, who made available the results of some of his own research into oral folklore; Colin Plen, who finally found something useful to do with that large storehouse of useless information; and Ingrid Jatho, for whom they need to redefine the word 'secretary'.

Special thanks also goes to all those people who provided me with raw material, whether intentionally or unintentionally. The latter includes, in particular, the *Sunday Times* and the *Star* newspapers. Long may they remain a haven for urban legends.

Intentional help came from Ike Motsapi, Harry Dugmore, Charles Leonard, Gwen Gill, Barry Ronge, David Barritt, Rico Schacherl, Bob Kernohan, Hanli Buber, Juliet Dear, Linda Dubery, Ted Botha, Jessie Araujo, Lydia Araujo, Jean Lack, Hilton Lack, Howard Dalton, Blaize Hopkinson, Megan Gill, Andy Gill,

Charmaine Naidoo, Peter Godson, Julie Beukes, Joyce Ozynski, Georgia Jammine, Jeanette Minnie, Denise Meyerson, Marion Sher, Alida Taylor, Neil Hendler, Marion Brower, Jacques Lack, Lana Jacobsen, Nicky Carter, Gilly Bright, Derick Botha and Krisjan Lemmer.

None of the above is credited for individual legends in the course of the book, as many of the tales came from several sources in identical variations. Exceptions are those who were responsible for specific published versions, or where specialist knowledge was involved.

Readers are welcome to send variations on the legends in this book, or 'new' legends, to me: Arthur Goldstuck, PO Box 93309, Yeoville 2143, South Africa.

214

REFERENCES

BOOKS:

The Automobile Association. *Off the Beaten Track.* The Motorist Publications, 1987.

Adams, Cecil. *The Straight Dope.* Ballantine Books, 1984.

Belloc, Hilaire. *Cautionary Verses.* Duckworth, 1940.

Brunvand, Jan Harold. *The Choking Doberman.* Penguin, 1984.

Brunvand, Jan Harold. *The Vanishing Hitchhiker.* Pan Books, 1983.

Goss, Michael. *The Evidence for Phantom Hitch-Hikers.* Aquarian Press with the Association for the Scientific Study of Anomalous Phenomena, 1984.

Miller, Penny. *Myths and Legends of Southern Africa.* Bulpin, 1979.

Poundstone, William. *Big Secrets.* Corgi Books, 1985.

Smith, Paul. *The Book of Nastier Legends.* Routledge & Kegan Paul, 1986.

NEWSPAPERS AND PRESS SERVICES:

Associated Press
Beeld
Capital Times
Citizen
City Press
Daily Mail
The Guardian
New Musical Express
Roodepoort Record

Saturday Star
The Star
Sunday Star
Sunday Times
Sunday Times Magazine
Vrye Weekblad
Washington Post
Weekend Post
Weekly Mail

MAGAZINES:

Bona

Crisis comic

Excellence

Fate

Kerkbode

People

Personality

Style

The Trend